Sarah Bartlett is a professional astrologer and author of internationally bestselling books such as *The Little Book of Practical Magic, The Tarot Bible, The Witch's Spellbook, The Secrets of the Universe in 100 Symbols* and *National Geographic Guide to the World's Supernatural Places*. Sarah practises natural magic, tarot, astrology and other esoteric arts in the heart of the countryside.

Sarah Bartlett

The Little Book of Earth Magic

Connect to the Magic
of the World around You

PIATKUS

PIATKUS

First published in Great Britain in 2021 by Piatkus

3 5 7 9 10 8 6 4

A CIP catalogue record for this book
is available from the British Library.

ISBN 978-0-3494-2809-3

Typeset in Perpetua by M Rules
Printed and bound in Great Britain by
Clays Ltd, Elcograf S.p.A.

Papers used by Piatkus are from well-managed forests
and other responsible sources.

MIX
Paper from
responsible sources
FSC® C104740

Piatkus
An imprint of
Little, Brown Book Group
Carmelite House
50 Victoria Embankment
London EC4Y 0DZ

An Hachette UK Company
www.hachette.co.uk

www.littlebrown.co.uk

To Jess, and all who believe in magic

Contents

PART THREE
Earth Connection Rituals

PART FOUR
Magical Practices, Charms and Spells

Introduction

Nature is filled with magic and this book is about connecting to that magic to help you fulfil your own desires and to give back goodness to this precious planet and restore its harmony.

In my early twenties, I was living in London when a charming friend of mine gave me a gift of two 'grimoires' he was about to chuck out. One was called *Le Petit Albert*, which was a popular book in eighteenth-century Europe that is still available today. It is packed with spells – ranging from how to catch a lover to simply how to catch a fish! The other book was rare and unpublished, more like a Book of Shadows, another type of grimoire, and dated from the end of the nineteenth century. Each parchment page was covered in penned incantations, scrawled symbols, fine pencil drawings, or filled with shrivelled pressed flowers and magic charms. There were drawings of landscapes, trees, intricate botanical studies and astrological and alchemical motifs.

On the inside cover of the second book, a beautiful arts and crafts-style bookplate read 'Ex libris Gaia'. At first, I didn't think too much about that name, but as I turned the pages, I began to feel as if it were maybe Mother Earth (Gaia) herself who had written this magic book. This curious Book of Shadows led me on a journey to connect to the magic in nature – and to share that with you in these pages.

There is such a wide variety of botanical ingredients available for Earth magic and for this book I have carefully chosen those that have well-known magical correspondences – whether in folklore, ancient practices or as modern-day healing tools. You will find a Glossary of Correspondences on page 297 to help you design your own spells. The most important ingredient of all, though, is your own connection with nature.

Your connection

Working with the magic of the Earth will reveal the ways in which you are unique and help you to discover how deep within you lies hidden potential, sacred to the journey you are taking here on Earth. Aligning to nature's magic will also enable you to manifest that potential inside yourself. The general idea of connecting to the magic of nature is perhaps best summed up in this affirmation, which you can repeat to yourself every day: 'When we are at one with nature, we are at one with our sacred selves; when we are at one with our sacred selves, we are at one with the Earth and its magic.'

It is humbling and gratifying to know that you are part of this universe and you have a right to follow your own path just by virtue of being born on this planet. In fact, as you will discover, the more you connect and relate to nature, embrace the bee, hug the tree, love the wild, watch the antics of the hare, the more you are engaging in your sacred self and the magic that is within you too . . .

PART ONE

Natural Wisdom

There are lots of ways to connect to the magic all around us in nature. We can simply go for a walk across the countryside or tend a garden, cast spells and perform ritual enchantments, write down sigils (special symbols), carry talismans or amulets, or set out sacred geometrical grids and perform sacred rites. Whatever type of magic you practise, as long as you are doing it for the good of yourself and for the good of the planet, and align yourself with the hidden powers of nature, then the magic will happen as you intend it to.

This part of the book will help you to ground yourself in the natural world by getting to know some of the deities and myths that are connected with it. We will also look at some fascinating facts about the Earth, before going on to discover the importance of the five elements in magic and how these relate to ourselves and the land around us.

You will find some simple yet powerful ways to strengthen your connection with nature and to understand your place in it, which will help to give your magic even stronger foundations. By becoming a guardian witch and working with Earth magic, you will discover how to help both yourself and the planet.

Chapter 1

Understanding Earth Magic

There are many different ways to practise magic, such as folk magic, high magic, sympathetic magic, divination and natural magic. Earth magic embraces all of these different branches, either in combination or on their own; for example, some spells rely heavily on natural magic, while others may include a little dash of folk, sympathetic or high magic to complement or enhance the intention or the outcome.

Here's a brief description of the some of the most common practices used in Earth magic:

Sympathetic magic uses corresponding objects, ideas, places or colours to help strengthen your wish or desire. For example, if you are looking for a new job, you might place a sunstone (for good luck) on your desk (a symbol of work) to amplify the Sun's power to shine on any employment situation.

Folk magic covers a range of practices that often draw on local superstitions and folklore, with a particular emphasis on working with herbs, flowers, plants and charms.

Divination uses specific tools such as tarot, palmistry and horoscopes to connect to universal knowledge. These practices can help you understand where you are in life and what you can do to improve your situation in relation to your past, present and future.

High magic involves performing special rituals usually according to specific cult rules or sets of spiritual practices. These can include incantations, chanting, dancing, drumming, or calling on deities or other supernatural powers for blessings and help.

Healing magic draws on the intuition, chakras, auras and the soul to connect to universal energy, and incorporates specific plants, potions, essential oils and crystals to invoke holistic healing.

Natural magic uses everything in nature – from flora and fauna to the elements, the stars, rocks and crystals – to connect to Earth energy and to enhance positive results, and it often incorporates some of the other types of magic too.

The nature of Earth magic

Natural Earth magic is very much a part of you, as you are part of nature's magic. In fact, by giving out goodness and making good things happen, you will help to restore good energy to the world and the universe. The more you believe in this powerful cycle of energy, the more it will work in your favour and benefit others too. However, the only way to make sure it works for you is to practise Earth magic and make a daily commitment to yourself and the planet, even if this is only for a few minutes each day.

Daily connection practice

Here follows a simple daily practice that will help you to keep in touch with the magic all around you, even if you are leading a hectic, urban lifestyle.

1. Sit down and relax for a moment, wherever you are. Close your eyes and listen to the sounds around you for a minute or two. Even

if you think you live in silence, you will begin to hear noise – maybe a distant car, a bird, the wind in the trees, a humming fridge. Be mindful of the different noises, and realise how sharp your hearing is and how the noises you hear are soundwaves emitting from some other thing, being or place, all of which are connecting to you.

2. Now, work with your sight. Open your eyes and focus on one spot in front of you, then let go of that focus, so that your peripheral vision takes over. You will begin to see more of what is around you. As you do so, repeat aloud: 'I am connected to nature both above and below, both the physical and the spiritual, and to the essence of the planet itself. I will nurture the magic of planet Earth, both within and without.'

3. Come out of your meditation when you are ready, and repeat the practice whenever you feel disconnected from the natural world.

Symbol and myth – uniting above with below

The more you engage in nature, either through imagery, imagination or close contact with it, the more you will feel you are connected to the Earth and that you are both sharing and restoring the magic of this planet. The use of symbols, archetypes and myths can all enrich your magical engagement with nature. So let's start with the ancient Greek myth of Persephone, the daughter of the fertility goddess Demeter, and discover how it relates to you in your magical practice.

The underworld god, Hades, was renowned for his sexual appetite and lusted after the fertility goddess Demeter's daughter, Persephone. In one of his more impulsive moments, Hades snatched Persephone from the upper world and took her to the underworld to be his consort. Grieving at the loss of her daughter, and determined to be avenged on Zeus (who, according to some accounts, had always promised Persephone to his brother Hades), Demeter brought an end to all fertility on Earth.

To save humanity from disaster, Zeus struck a deal with Demeter that Persephone would spend six months in the underworld and six months in the upper world. Hades agreed to Zeus' demands, because he knew Persephone would always return to him in winter as she had eaten six pomegranate seeds from his garden, binding her to him forever. In this way, Persephone became responsible for the changing seasons and the eternal cycle of growth, harvest, decay and renewal. Her six months with Hades was the time of winter, sterile, dark and dormant, until the spring when she rejoined her mother and brought the world to life again. This myth was also celebrated in the famous Greek Eleusinian

Mysteries, secret rites performed in early spring and autumn by initiates who sought eternal life. They were believed to be derived from an ancient agrarian cult of the Mycenean period.

Persephone is, then, a bit of a paradox, in that she brings us light, growth and the spring, but also takes us into the dark of winter. Similarly, in Earth magic, you must work with the natural cycles and cast spells according to time, place and need. Persephone's underworld is a symbol of the deepest part of you, the sacred you and your secret garden filled with pomegranates – the fruits of beauty, fertility and eternal life. When you practise magic, you are connecting this deepest part of you to the daylight world of nature as well.

Persephone's underworld kingdom is also a motif for the hidden places within the Earth itself: its caverns, deep ocean trenches, underground tunnels, water courses, fabulous crystals, diamonds, fossils and other riches found within bedrock and geological strata. And it relates to what begins beneath ground – such as the roots of trees, plants, the formation of crystals, seeds that burst into life, worms who cast and turn the soil to make it richer – and then pushes back up into the light to recycle the hidden energy and bring back life again.

So what has this all to do with you and Earth magic? By simply working with these natural cycles, by being inspired by nature, and reviving and caring for it, by planting your intention, sowing your desire, and at times finding stillness, at others potency, and by moving between two worlds of the outer you and the inner you (and therefore being at one with two aspects of the Earth — 'above' and 'below'), you will discover how to be a guardian witch and enrich not only yourself with goodness but the planet as well.

Chapter 2

Earth Facts and Folklore

It's great fun to practise Earth magic, but some fundamental knowledge will help you to better understand the energy that you are working with and how to use it well. This chapter will provide you with information to help you both appreciate the Earth and where it came from, and know more about what you are dealing with when you engage with nature. These insights will help you to become a wiser guardian witch of our precious planet.

A few facts about the Earth

Our planet is an extraordinary wonder, yet many people have been driven to exploit it for profit or desire (both of which are manifestations of our deepest survival needs). Since the dawning of humankind, we have taken liberally from the Earth, but neglected to give back in return. Here are some fascinating facts about the planet we call home, which show just how special and unique it is.

The Earth's origins

Although there are various theories about how the solar system came into being, the most widely accepted model is known as 'the Nebular hypothesis'. This theory proposes that around 4.5 billion years ago, part of a molecular cloud made up of dust and gas began to collapse. The resulting gravitational compression created the Sun at the centre of a rotating disc of dust and gases, which formed the planets, moons and other celestial bodies such as meteoroids. One of these planets is the Earth. Although similar to Venus and Mercury in structure, Earth is the only planet with surface water.

The structure of the Earth

The Earth is made up of an outer solid crust, beneath which is a layer of rocky mantle and, deep within that, a core. The outer crust is on average nineteen miles deep and made up of rock such as granite and basalt. Below this sits the upper mantle, which is divided into moving plates that constantly grind, separate or collide against each other, sometimes resulting in earthquakes. The inner mantle is a layer of hot, sticky, viscous molten rock, while the innermost core is made up of iron and nickel metals. The liquid, outer layer of the central core generates the Earth's geomagnetic field.

Geology

On the Earth's surface, there are volcanoes, mountains, valleys, and deep ravines – not forgetting oceans, hills, rivers, Polar Regions, flat plains and vast deserts. The average depth of the world's oceans is about 2.5 miles deep, and most of the world's volcanoes are hidden under them. The Earth's longest mountain range is also underwater and forms a chain between the bottom of the Arctic and Atlantic oceans.

The Earth's oceans

Earth is special because it is the only planet on which the majority of the surface is covered by vast oceans – 71 per cent, to be exact. This created the perfect environment for life to evolve around 3.8 billion years ago. Sadly, some of the features and inhabitants of our beautiful seas, such as coral reefs, mangroves, giant turtles, penguins and other polar species, are under threat due to the effects of climate change and other forms of human intervention. This is why it is so important to cherish and nurture our oceans and marine life.

Electromagnetic energy

Some say the magical, invisible essence of nature is perhaps the same thing as electromagnetic energy. This is a force field released into space by stars such as the Sun (sunlight, rainbows and ultraviolet light are all manifestations of electromagnetic energy). On Earth, forms of electromagnetic energy include radio and TV waves, radar, heat in the guise of infrared radiation, light, X-rays, microwaves (i.e. a form of radiation, rather than the kitchen appliance) and gamma rays. It is believed among esoteric circles that electromagnetic energy is perhaps aligned to the so-called 'aura' of all life on Earth. It may be that this energy is actually the invisible life force of the cosmos, animating all things.

Auras and magnetism

The renowned sixteenth-century Swiss alchemist and physician Paracelsus believed that a vital force emanated from the human body as an envelope of light. More recently this has come to be known as the aura. The word 'aura' comes from Greek, meaning 'air' or 'breeze'.

In the eighteenth century, Austrian physicist Franz Anton Mesmer devised a theory that the universe was filled with an invisible magnetic fluid that connected all living things. He believed this energy, which he called 'animal magnetism', could be manipulated by a person in a technique that came to be known as mesmerism, enabling that person to exert a powerful influence over other people's actions, thoughts and feelings.

Today, scientists agree that plants convert carbon

dioxide into glucose in a process called photosynthesis, in which oxygen is a by-product; whereas when humans and animals breathe, we expel carbon dioxide and take in molecular oxygen. The air around any plant is likely to be rich in oxygen and the air around any person is likely to be rich in CO_2, so the exchange of these compounds while we are talking to plants or trees is actually mutually beneficial. This is when scientific magic starts to happen. Whether we call them a magnetic field, an aura or an exchange of energy, these sorts of forces appear to be similar to the mystical or spiritual view of there being an invisible essence that pervades all.

The Gaia hypothesis

The Gaia hypothesis, first proposed by the British chemist, environmentalist and futurist James Lovelock (b.1919), and co-developed with microbiologist Lynn Margulis in the 1970s, states that living organisms and inorganic material are part of a dynamic system that shapes the Earth's biosphere, and maintains the Earth's positive environment. (Lovelock named his hypothesis after our friendly ancient Greek Earth goddess, Gaia; see page 20.) In more recent approaches, the Earth has been viewed as a self-regulating organism, and this hypothesis has been embraced since the 1990s by environmentalists as part of a heightened awareness of ecological and climate change issues. Gaia appears to be at the core of the planet's ecosystem, and also at the core of its magic.

Why is our planet called Earth?

Ancient peoples named the planets in the solar system after various deities. The Romans, for example, named the planets that lie closest to us Mercury, Venus and Mars, but as they believed the Earth to be the centre of the universe, they saw little reason to name it as though it were another body in the sky. In pagan Europe, our world was usually referred to as Terra Mata, or Mother Earth. The English word 'Earth' was not used for our home planet until the beginning of the fifteenth century CE. The word 'Earth' derives from an eighth-century Anglo-Saxon word *erda* or *erde*, meaning ground or soil, and is rooted in turn in the Indo-European word *er*, meaning 'Earth' or 'ground'.

Lore, myth and magic

In relation to the Earth and nature, there exists a long history of legends, folklore, spiritual ideas and mythological connections – enough to fill a book of its own. Most legends that arose around specific gods were popularised to enable people to recall and live in accordance with their specific belief system. In Greek mythology, Zeus was the god of the heavens, Gaia was Mother Earth and Hades the god of the underworld. In Celtic mythology, the goddess Abnoba was associated with forests and rivers, while the bear goddess Artio presided over the wilderness. The Horned God, Cernunnos, was responsible for fertility, stags, serpents and dogs. He was sometimes represented as the Green Man, a popular figure in both Christian churches and folklore, who had long been associated with the Earth, and may have been assimilated from more ancient nature deities such as Dionysus in Greek mythology and his Roman counterpart Bacchus, or Osiris in Egyptian mythology (often shown with a 'green' face) – and not forgetting the Norse god Odin.

Gaia

In ancient Greek mythology, Gaia was a primordial deity who rose out of chaos to become the mother of Ouranos, the sky or heaven. With Ouranos, she bore the Titans, who became the parents of many of the Olympian gods, the Cyclopes and the giants; and with her son Pontus, the sea, she gave birth to primordial sea gods such as Nereus and Ceto. Worshipped as a 'giver of gifts' and also believed to be the source of the god Apollo's oracular power, Gaia has been acknowledged by many as Mother Earth, the physical embodiment of the Earth, and seen as its goddess.

Mother Nature

The word 'nature' comes from the Latin word *natura*, meaning 'birth' or 'character'. The personification of Mother Nature, originating in Gaia's identification as Mother Earth, became widely popular in medieval folklore in Europe. Christian thinkers were meanwhile attempting to propagate the notion that 'nature' was in fact created by God, and rejected the popularised version of Mother Nature. However, the esoteric and pagan traditions of ancient Greece and Rome survived underground, and Mother Nature continued to endure as an empowering image in the mind of artists, poets and writers from the Renaissance onwards.

Earth mother goddess

In many cultures, the Earth mother goddess was a fertility deity. The Aztecs knew her as Tonantzin, meaning 'our mother'; to the Incas, she was Pachamama, 'Mother Earth' or 'Mother Universe', who also presided over planting and harvesting; while the Chinese referred to her as Houtu, 'Queen of the Earth'. In Hinduism, she is worshipped as Bhuma Devi, and in Norse mythology she appears as the goddess Jord (sometimes known simply as Earth). Among the indigenous peoples of America, she is known as Nokomis, the Grandmother. In Algonquian legend, Earth Mother lives beneath the clouds, while to the Pawnee peoples the Earth goddess Atira manifests as corn. Despite Earth itself being personified as a deity, nature was considered a mysterious force and later became associated with animism.

Animism

What is animism? Well, put simply, it is the belief that an invisible universal energy flows through everything – from a stone to a cloud and a human being to a plant. Animism was first referred to in a spiritual sense by German physicist Georg Ernst Stahl (1660–1734) and used by anthropologist Sir Edward Burnett Tylor in 1871 in his theory of the universal animation of nature. The word comes from the Latin *animus* or *anima*, which is rooted in the Indo-European word for 'breath'. The animistic spiritual belief is that everything is permeated by 'spirit', 'soul' or 'the breath of life', also known as *prana* in Hinduism and *ch'i* in Taoist philosophy. Tylor argued that the belief in there being a spirit or soul in everything was the most primitive principle of all religions.

Personifications of nature

If ancient peoples believed in the existence of magic all around them, whether in plant life, trees or the landscape, then it wasn't long before they personified these invisible forces too. The essential quality of a tree became a god or a nymph in classical mythology, as did the essence of the land in other cultures. In Chinese mythology, every village, city, field or farm was believed to have its own *Tudi Gong*, an elemental Earth spirit. There were also spirits known as *Kuei Shen*, nature spirits, who might inhabit a tree, live by a stream or preside over a garden. In India, the Hindu god Himavat was the lord of the Himalayas, and fathered Ganga, the goddess of the River Ganges. In Navajo mythology, the trickster god Coyote was responsible for the rain.

Although most ancient people's spiritual practice was based on polytheism, i.e. the belief in many gods, the idea of there being an animating spirit lay at the core of many traditions – from Alaskan and Canadian Inuit traditions, to the Shinto beliefs of Japan. These beliefs merged with the worship of nature spirits and ancestors.

In most Native American indigenous communities, animals, plants, the elements and the landscape are all given equal respect. These traditions believe in a connection between all living things, as well as the rocks, sand, sea and Earth. Each local community adapted their beliefs according to their geographical needs. For example, the indigenous peoples of the Great Plains practised daily rituals to worship the Sun and the great sky; while those who cultivated the land, such as the Creek peoples of the Southeastern United States, worshipped the agricultural deity Corn Woman. According to Native American writer Professor John Mohawk, 'Nature informs us and it is our obligation to read nature as you would a book, to feel nature as you would a poem, to touch nature as you would yourself, to be part of that.'

Folk traditions

For centuries, herbs and plants have been used for remedies, potions, healing aids, cures and medicines. Ancient knowledge was passed down orally in the form of recipes, as well as tried and tested concoctions. In Europe, many country folk who had such knowledge were accused of witchcraft, heresy or of being in league with demons. From the middle of the sixteenth to eighteenth centuries, witch hunts reached a peak, and folk magic became synonymous with witchcraft. The powerful correspondence between a herbal remedy and the art of divination, for example, was considered heretical, and meant most magic practitioners had no choice but to continue their work in secret for fear of being burned at the stake. Among communities where indigenous beliefs still held sway until the arrival of European colonisation, the power of nature continued to thrive in their traditions, and their secrets were kept safe.

Through the information, guidance and magic in this book, the delights of the Earth will be yours to shape, share and graciously use for your own well-being, and most importantly, to bless all who belong here with the grace and sacredness of nature's magic.

Chapter 3

The Five Elements of Earth Magic

In this book, I will often be referring to the five elements of Earth magic, and show you how to use ingredients associated with each of these elements to boost your own connection to nature. The five elements used in magic are often depicted in the form of a pentagram, and were particularly favoured for use in their practice by the Hermetic Order of the Golden Dawn. (The Order's founder member, Edward E. Waite, is renowned for his development of the Rider-Waite-Smith tarot deck, in which the pentagram appears as one of the suits.) The pentagram or five-pointed star – also known as a pentacle when the star is surrounded by a circle – is a symbol also used by Wiccans and other Neopagan belief systems, as well as by the Freemasons and the likes of the Renaissance occultist and astrologer Cornelius Agrippa.

What are the five elements?

In many spiritual practices, such as Ayurveda and Vedic teachings, everything in nature is believed to be made up of five elemental energies. By working with these, we can achieve harmony within ourselves and a connection to the magic of the Earth, although the elements may go by different names in different systems. For example, in yoga the five elements are known as Air, Fire, Water, Earth and Space; while in Chinese astrology and its off-shoot feng shui, the five elements are Fire, Earth, Water, Metal and Wood.

In Western magic, four of the elements correspond to the compass points – north, south, east and west – and relate to the elements of astrology, which are Earth, Fire, Air and Water. The fifth element, often known as the quintessential element, Quintessence or Spirit, unifies the four. The elements have particular correspondences in nature (as described below), while the fifth element, Spirit, unifies them all. Spirit is you, the practitioner.

By working with the five elements, you will evoke the

right balance of energy in your life and also in nature. Throughout the rituals, spells and practices in this book, you will find traditional folk ingredients, symbolic elements, sigils and talismans that correspond to each of the five elements to help you connect easily to the magic of the world around you. Here are the five elements and some key associations:

The element of Earth – flora and fauna

The element of Earth relates to flora and fauna. In this context, 'flora' refers to all plant life, which means there is an endless choice of ingredients when working with this element. In the practices in this book, you can always replace anything that's difficult to find with an associated ingredient by referring to the list in the Glossary of Correspondences on page 297. Likewise, for the category of fauna there is an abundance of animal life, so I have kept to the most well-established or well-known symbolic associations. You can, of course, create your own symbolic interpretations.

The element of Fire – landscape

The element of Fire relates to the landscape, which is often overlooked as a magical ingredient. Symbolically, valleys are usually associated with fertility and comfort, while deserts represent emptiness, lack and drought. But the desert has other meanings too: its extremes of temperature can reflect our own moods, while its lack of rain may symbolise our thirst for knowledge. The valley, for all its nurturing power, also has darker associations, such as emotional overload or being in thrall to the power of others. Working with the landscape means you can open your eyes and literally look at a symbol before you – and perhaps even search beyond the horizon.

The element of Air – sky and stars

The element of Air relates to the sky and stars. Beyond the Earth, but still connected to us, is the sky. The sky is filled with amazing symbols that have been used for centuries for divination and magic. The sky is made up of the solar system, the constellations, infinity and beyond. But the sky is also about the weather, the clouds, the atmosphere, the sunsets and sunrises. The sky and stars allow us to wonder, to live in awe and to realise that the universe is much greater than us. The unpredictable nature of weather patterns and their effect on us can remind us that Mother Nature cares little for who we are, yet still embraces us in Her arms. She can send storms, tsunamis and tornadoes to wreak havoc on and destroy communities, yet She can also bring rain to save us from drought or warm sunshine to stir the first snowdrops into life. In a way, we are Mother Nature's children and must respect Her power, realising that She can teach us more than we know if we let Her.

The element of Water – sacred places

The element of Water relates to sacred places. In the same way, sacred spirituality, the soul and the unconscious all correspond to Water. There are also specific places in the world that have become associated with a sacred energy and thus have become epicentres for spirituality; vortexes for supernatural energy or portals to a mystical other-world. These places include the Great Pyramids, some lakes, mountains, earthworks, standing stones, ley lines, sacred caves and certain monuments. Whether created by humanity or not, they are significant in that they have become part of the natural world around us, reflecting civilisations or peoples who believed in their own forms of magic or religion.

The element of Spirit – you

So where do you fit into the elemental sacred world? That's easy to answer – just by virtue of being born on this planet you are already innately blessed with magical power. You are the generating Spirit of the pentagram, and it is you who will harness the magic of the four other elements to create harmony and well-being for yourself and nature.

Simply follow the practices described in this book and you will become more aware of how all things are connected. If you can see that you are part of the natural world and nature is part of you, then you are well on your way to becoming a guardian witch. But before you leap into the art of practising Earth magic, let's pause to think a little bit more about nature's cycles . . .

Nature's cycles

Understanding nature's cycles and when to utilise them will help you to see how you are part of the bigger picture and how to connect to the magic of these cycles to maximise your practical work.

Lunar cycles

Magic work is often performed in harmony with the Moon's cycles simply because these cycles are the most consistent (apart from those of the Sun) when viewed from our geocentric viewpoint. For magical purposes, the lunar cycle begins with the New Crescent Moon, followed by the Waxing Moon, the Full Moon, the Waning Moon, and the Dark of the Moon.

Each lunar phase has a particular type of energy; for example, a Waxing Moon has the same energy of growth as spring, so springtime or during a Waxing Moon would be the best time to perform spells or rituals designed to create, flourish and promote; whereas a Full Moon has the same energy as midsummer, making this a moment to complete a project or finalise a deal. A Waning Moon equates to autumn, and ushers in a period for reflection, planning and the decluttering of our hearts or minds.

Here's a brief rundown of how to use each phase of the Moon wisely for your own magical purposes:

New Crescent Moon Perfect energy for spells and rituals concerned with fresh ideas, creative goals, new romance, fertility, new beginnings, communicating, artistic inspiration and spiritual revival.

Waxing Moon This lunar phase will help you to perform spells to maximise any creative inclinations, put thoughts into action, develop or promote your goals, reinforce or make it clear where you're going in a new relationship, and help you be open about your needs and desires.

Full Moon A time for culmination, for finishing something off that you've already started, finalising a project, or committing to a relationship or business deal, tying up loose ends, or confirming a future goal.

Waning Moon A period for letting go of the past and banishing bad thoughts. It is also the perfect time to give up bad habits or to try to kick an addiction.

Dark of the Moon This is when we're unable to see the Moon. During this period you can perform spells for meditation, emotional healing, understanding your deeper self, or for spiritual connection.

Throughout this book you will find spells or rituals specifically aligned to the different lunar phases.

The Sun's cycles
Some of practices in this book ask you to work with the cycles of the Sun. There are some similarities between the Sun cycles and the lunar cycles; for example, when the Sun rises, this is the same sort of energy as that of the Waxing Moon or spring; the midday Sun is symbolic of the summer solstice or the Full Moon; we can associate sunset with a Waning Moon or the end of autumn; and the midnight Sun with the winter solstice or the Dark

of the New Moon. By understanding and noticing the correspondences between these cycles, you can find the appropriate times to maximise the success of particular magical practices.

The changing seasons

We all notice the changing seasons and how winter gives way to spring, or the summer to autumn, and the effect of this on the landscape around us. But do you ever stop and contemplate what this means for nature – or for you? Do you feel any connection to those changing cycles? Subject to your local climate and environment, noticing how the seasons change and adapting your life accordingly is an important step to being at one with the planet. When it rains, appreciate it; when it snows, wonder at it; when it's hot and sunny, accept the solar energy that gives us life; when spring comes, welcome Persephone's return to the upper world (see page 11); and when autumn comes, celebrate the Harvest Moon and be ready to embrace the dark soul of winter.

The cycle of life

Our own life cycle seems short in comparison to that of an ancient oak tree or even the planet itself, while the eternal cycle of day and night acts as a reminder of the soul's cycle too – particularly if you believe in the Neoplatonic idea that the soul begins its existence as a star in the sky, comes to Earth, and then returns to the sky as a star until it is reborn on Earth again. When we connect with nature, even shorter life cycles than our own – such as those of a mayfly, moth or morning glory flower – remind us that life is as long as it is meant to be, and that the Earth itself is part of the greater cycles of the universe and beyond, which we have yet to understand.

Our own inner cycles and landscapes

Whatever gender we are, we all have cycles, rhythms – a flow of life that like the tide washes back and forth across the physical self, our very own beach. Our life cycle is the greatest one of these; then there's our daily cycle of sleep and wakefulness, the menstrual cycle, biorhythms and so on. We may also have spiritual or emotional cycles. Similarly, we can learn to adapt to the cycles of our cultural background and the landscape of our geographical location, and how this changes depending on whether it's night or day.

Your perception of your physical surroundings is a crucial reflection of your inner landscape. An awareness of which features you are drawn to, admire or find inspiring in your urban or countryside surroundings will enable you to understand a little more about your own inner landscape and how you can connect and align to the goodness that you perceive is right for you. For example, if you love the mountains, then your spiritual self will be boosted and balanced if you work and live within a mountainous landscape. Or you might find greatest pleasure by the sea, so to improve your connection to nature you might find you need to move to a seaside town.

To bring our inner self or inner landscape into balance with the outer world, even if we are unable to physically inhabit the landscape we most love, we can help ourselves by incorporating relevant symbols, imagery, holidays, spellwork or rituals into our lives, and in this way maximise that outer landscape energy and bring well-being to our inner landscape and spiritual self.

Simple ways to connect with nature

The more you are at one with the Earth, the more easily you can harness its energy, and feel protected and nurtured by it. To get started, here are some simple ways to engage with nature.

Foraging

The word 'forage' is rooted in the old French word *forrage*, meaning fodder for horses and cattle. Foraging for natural ingredients is one of the simplest ways to engage with nature. This will depend on your local environment, but set out with the intention of finding something that you can use in your spellwork. For example, if you live near the sea, you could comb the beach for shells, stones or driftwood or fill up a phial with seawater. If you live near woods or forests, you can go in search of fallen leaves, buds or twigs. If you need herbs, you could forage for them in your garden or hedgerows, using a field guide for safe identification. However, avoid picking wildflowers and rare plants, as these are more precious when left in nature than on your kitchen table. Whatever your local habitat, think about what is available; and if you are creating your own rituals, adjust your ingredients accordingly. Foraging will help you to engage with plants, trees and other botanicals – in fact, simply walking barefoot on the grass or touching the bark of a tree counts as 'foraging for contact' with nature too.

Planting and gardening

It doesn't matter whether you have a garden or just a small planter – as long as you have a small patch of soil, you can grow herbs, flowers and other plants that will be superb ingredients for rituals and magic. When growing your own plants, think about when would be the best time to plant these, and whether to use seeds, established seedlings or plug plants. For me, sowing seeds, tending to them and watching them grow is the most liberating and rewarding experience.

You can also sow seeds in the wild and return precious wildflowers or botanicals to their natural landscapes to re-energise the local habitat. But make sure you research which plants will work in which area and avoid upsetting the local habitat by introducing unsuitable seedlings or invasive species.

Similarly, gardening – whether turning the soil for a plot of vegetables, mowing the lawn, or simply watering and tending to a few pot plants – offers a simple way to advance the joy of planting into a ritual in itself. If you nurture your space with loving care and dedicated spiritual energy, this will ensure that your garden grows both physically and metaphorically, and with it your alignment to nature.

Create a daisy chain

Although we have to be really cautious about picking wildflowers, particularly endangered species, there are a few species which you can seek out to make yourself a crown of flowers to enhance spring or summer rituals. Daisy chains are easy to make and as you sit among them to weave your crown, you will feel as light-hearted and bright as a daisy itself.

Wild-watching

Wild animals are sacred, and observing and watching them, taking time to understand their habits, movements, life cycles and their very essence, will align you to the quintessential nature of the universe too. Even if you can only watch a few birds feeding in your garden or local park, you can still observe their behaviour, hear their tweeting, acknowledge their presence and appreciate their innate beauty. Be thankful and gracious for these precious moments and show your appreciation by lighting a candle when you return home to thank the planet for sharing its riches.

Walking and other outdoor activities

Adventure holidays, camping – not forgetting glamping – and other countryside pursuits are currently enjoying something of a renaissance. As I touched on earlier, aligning yourself spiritually to a ridge of mountains or the depths of the ocean is a fantastic way to engage with nature. Whether you're a rambler, hiker, stroller or beachcomber, a climber, a bike fanatic or simply want to swim in an ocean, all forms of outdoor activities will help to improve your connection with nature – as long as you remember to be aware of what is around you.

Even walking can be a superb meditational tool. It doesn't matter how long you walk for, be it ten minutes or three hours. Walking mediation is actually one of the best ways to meditate. All you need to do is count your steps in your mind and be conscious and mindful of the world around you as you go.

Getting ready to practise Earth magic

Now that you have started to strengthen your connection with nature and its cycles, Part 2 will tell you all you need to know about the basic ingredients and the practice of Earth magic. However, before we move on, there are some things to consider.

First, why are you practising Earth magic? It's time to ask yourself the following questions and answer truthfully from your deepest self:

- Do I love the natural world?
- Do I want to feel a better connection to it?
- Do I care for nature and all there is on this planet?

- Am I prepared to be a guardian witch and radiate as much goodness as I receive?
- Am I willing to share my magical practice with the universe?

If you answered 'yes' to all of these questions, then you have already made the most important decision – and that is to engage with the Earth. There is just one more consideration to keep in mind, and that is that you must make a choice to believe and practise what you believe. It's no good half-heartedly using this book without believing in the magic you are going to create.

RITUAL FOR INTENTION, BELIEF AND PURPOSE

Before you start gathering, collecting, foraging or working with visual references or real ingredients, please do the following exercise to confirm your good intentions. This is an exercise which calms and stills the mind, and will take you into a receptive yet giving place, a place where you can be at one with nature.

You will need:

1 white tea-light candle
pen
journal (or Book of Shadows if you have one)

1. Light a tea-light candle to invoke a sense of calm.
2. Sit cross-legged and rest your hands on your knees, and feel your hip bones anchoring you to the Earth.
3. Close your eyes and settle into a relaxed state. Become aware of your breathing. Take a deep breath in and a deep breath out. Continue to do this for several breaths. As you continue, concentrate on your intention to connect to the natural world; allow yourself to be enriched by it and try to give out goodness too.
4. Next, repeat in your mind the following verse:

   'My sacred soul connected now,
   To Earth this truth I show,
   To sing with birds, to love each cloud,
   Brings goodness all around.'

5. Stay settled for a few minutes in this place of contentment and sincerity to show your intentions are true, and that you believe in the magic of the Earth.
6. Open your eyes, and blow out the candle. You are now ready to make magic happen.
7. Repeat this simple verse whenever you set out to forage for ingredients, cast a spell, connect with the divine in nature, or simply engage in the natural world. You could write it down in your journal or Book of Shadows, illustrate it, or stick it on your wall, your desk, the inside

of your loo door, or in your bathroom mirror to remind you every day of your connection to Earth magic and to amplify your connection to nature.

PART TWO

The Nature of the Earth

The wealth of the natural world is all around us, and we are blessed to have so many ingredients at our fingertips. Yet it is possible to feel overwhelmed by the sheer abundance afforded to us when we wish to work magic. Remember that you don't have to rush out and try to experience all these things at once. Take your time. When you wish to work with natural ingredients, set your intention with the Ritual for Intention, Belief and Purpose on page 38, awaken your senses and take only what you need to work your magic.

You may enjoy imagining your magical ingredients or using symbolic imagery, but there is nothing like the 'real thing' to connect to the world around you. Make it your intention to touch a leaf, watch a grasshopper leap, stroke the fur of a cat, or listen to the sound of the surf. Whatever you do will remind you of your sacred, natural self – that you are sacred and natural too.

Chapter 4

Opening the Senses

We have seen how every flower, plant, animal or stone is animated with its own energy (see page 17), whether that is the electromagnetic force of a crystal or simply the life force of a butterfly. With belief and practice, we can harness and amplify these energies both for the good of ourselves and the planet.

These sorts of energy are best experienced through our six senses. Once you are attuned to all of your senses (including your deepest intuitive one), magic will come more naturally to you. Here are some simple suggestions to help you open yourself up and resonate with the magical energies found in nature.

Resonance

In nature, resonance is neither good nor bad, it just is. If we want to resonate with nature, to feel in tune with it in a positive way, we need to listen to its messages with care and attention, and be gracious in accepting that its power may be greater than ours. The following experiences will help you to understand and better connect to the energy of nature before you start to use her sacred powers. Just settle into these practices with a sense of wonder, curiosity and an open mind.

EXPERIENCE THE SOUND OF BIRDSONG

Listening to the sounds of nature offers an immediate relationship to the Earth. This little practice will enable you to enjoy resonance through the sounds in nature and to open your ears to its splendour.

1. You will need to find an outside space, where birds are likely to be. The species of bird doesn't matter; you might happen upon a familiar blackbird, a cooing wood pigeon, a fabulous thrush or a noisy

gang of rooks. It's a way of hearing things differently and not the sound itself which is important.

2. Make yourself comfortable, close your eyes and listen. Try to hear different frequencies, high notes, low notes, shrill ones or tuneless ones. Which sounds do you like? Which don't you like? When you reach a point where you can listen without making value judgements, then you are truly 'resonating' with the sound.

3. Birdsong is birdsong; it is neither good nor bad. Listening to the sounds of nature is like listening to your own voice and being objective enough to know that it's magical in itself. So once you have listened long enough to the birds, sing to them, talk to them. Listen to yourself speaking or singing and resonate with your own voice.

EXPERIENCE THE TOUCH OF FLOWERS

This simple practice offers a joyful encounter with plants.

You will need:

1 small bunch of herbs (lavender and rosemary work well, although you can choose any you like)
a handful of flora (rose petals are a lovely option, but use any flowers you prefer)

1. Combine the herbs with the flora and place them in the palm of your hand.

2. Sit back quietly, close your eyes and notice the feeling of the plants on your skin. Concentrate on this feeling – you may need to sit with it for three to five minutes before you begin to develop a new sense of touch, one that you have perhaps never experienced before. This is the magic of the energy that flows through all things.

3. Ask yourself: what does it feel like? Is it cold, warm, rippling, stimulating, itchy, calming or irritating? How you process the sensation will depend on your mood or energy, which is why you need to be in an open but mindful place when you are performing magic. Receptive but giving, aware but contained. Be aware of your reactions, and with growing awareness of those, you will experience a growing awareness of your relationship to nature.

EXPERIENCE THE FRAGRANCE OF ESSENTIAL OIL

Awakening your sense of smell will allow you to connect to the olfactory world around you. So when you next walk through a forest you will be alive to the smell of dampness, the woodiness of tree bark, or when you walk along a beach you can smell the salt or marine essences such as seaweed.

You will need:

1 drop of essential oil (ylang-ylang is preferable,
    but if you can't obtain this, choose an
    oil you like)

1. Sit on the floor with your legs crossed, or on a
    comfortable chair. As you inhale, count 'one',
    then exhale; count 'two' on the next breath you
    inhale, then exhale and so on. Do this until you
    have counted ten breaths in and out.
2. Now you're ready to inhale the beauty of your
    essential oil. Place a drop of the oil on a tissue,
    then shake the tissue in the air to diffuse the fra-
    grance. (Some essential oils can irritate the skin,
    so you may want to dilute the oil in a spoonful of
    water first to minimise its effect.)
3. Put your nose near the tissue and breathe in. As
    you do so, think about what the fragrance means
    to you; what memory or thought does it evoke? Is
    it sweet, erotic, sensuous or warm? Does it make
    you feel anything special? Enjoy the experience of
    your sense of smell.

EXPERIENCE YOUR SENSE OF SIGHT WITH THE SKY AND STARS

What better way is there to experience the stars and the
planets than to gaze at them in the night sky? This might

be tricky if you live in an area with light pollution or where the nights are often cloudy, but you can still usually catch a glimpse of the Full Moon. However, most of us don't look up at the sky very much, except when we are bothered by a passing plane or a flock of birds, or unless we are waiting for rainfall, spot a rainbow, or open our arms in a Sun salutation! This exercise can be carried out during the day or at night. It will encourage you to look at the sky more, whether to see the stars and the Moon, or simply to experience the joy of cloud-watching.

1. If you can find a place to lie down flat on your back and gaze at the sky, then so much the better. If you have no access to outside space, take a favourite image of the sky and lie down on the floor on a yoga mat or anything comfy. Hold up the image above you and concentrate on it.

2. If you are looking at a cloudy expanse of sky, you might be able to make out shapes, faces, animals, plants, letters, life, signs and symbols. Watch them pass, change shape and disappear, or come in and out of your focus.

3. If you have chosen to gaze at the stars, try to make out the difference between the planets and stars. Planets don't usually twinkle, whereas many stars do as they are so far away that there is a lot of atmospheric interference. If you lie in the same place long enough, you will begin to realise that the world is rotating (the illusion of course being that the constellations are revolving around us

on Earth). Enjoy your encounter with the sky, and realise that the infinite space above you is within you too.

EXPERIENCE YOUR MAGICAL, INTUITIVE SELF WITH CRYSTALS

Your magical, intuitive self is hidden deep within you and can connect you to nature's empowering energy to help you truly understand your deepest desires. (If you are working indoors, you may need to clear the energy of your sacred space first; see page 58.)

You will need:

1 white tea-light candle
1 piece of obsidian
1 large pebble or stone

1. Light and place the white tea-light candle somewhere where you can sit comfortably and safely before it. Next, place the obsidian to the right of the candle, and the stone to the left of it.
2. Close your eyes and try to establish a connection with the magic of nature. To do so, imagine that you're placing something sacred under the obsidian: what is it that you've hidden? A secret message, a charm or a spell? A gold ring, a leaf, or a flower? The choices are endless, but it's important to pick

something that will strengthen your connection to the Earth's innate goodness.

3. Now, imagine that what you seek is hidden under the pebble. Is it love, success, spiritual growth, or perhaps happiness?

4. Say aloud the two things that you've visualised under the stones, for example: 'I hide a leaf and I seek happiness.'

5. If you then go out and hide a leaf, you will open yourself up to happiness. You will also discover that your deepest intuitive self starts to connect to nature's magic too.

EXPERIENCE TREE CONNECTION

Finally, to awaken your magical senses, you need to experience all five elements (see chapter 3) as one magical connection. You can do this through talking to trees. Yes, I said it! Talk to trees and experience the power of your magical words!

1. Find a tree that seems to have been rooted for a long time in the ground in a quiet spot. An ancient oak, birch, ash or cedar would work well, as their energies have long been associated with magical power.

2. Stand beneath the tree and gently raise your hands to touch its trunk. Close your eyes and touch the bark. Think about how this feels for a few minutes

and then open your eyes, step back and address the tree as if it were your friend: 'Today, my friend, I have this to say . . . ' This is your opportunity to share whatever's on your mind with the tree. It might be the sort of thing you say to your best friend. Say it aloud – if you want to be private, it's fine to whisper – as words are magical and create the spell to resolve your intention.

3. Once you have shared your thoughts with the tree, smile at it. You may discover that if you do this often, the trees begin to speak back to you. Perhaps not in the same language, but in the other, magical way that you are beginning to understand.

Chapter 5

Preparing to Embrace Magic

Although it's fun to leap into practising spells and rituals with every intention of doing good for yourself and all around you, it's wise to prepare yourself so that you can take your magical art to a new level. Here are some simple rituals that will get you in the mood and allow you to incorporate natural Earth magic rituals into your daily life, helping you to feel that you're truly a guardian witch of planet Earth.

Creating a sacred altar

Your home is sacred to you so when you can't get outside to perform spells or rituals, it's important to have your own space that you can use for your magic work – this could be a table, a shelf or even a window ledge, as long as it works for you. Your indoor altar is also a place to meditate and reflect on your relationship with nature. To consecrate your altar before you begin using it, you can perform the following ritual:

You will need:

A small handful of basil leaves

1. Pick a night during a Waxing Moon phase to carry out this ritual. Take your small handful of basil leaves and brush them slowly across the surface of your altar. Repeat this movement five times, repeating the following words as you do so: 'This altar is cleansed of all that is negative. In this space I will find my true connection to nature.'
2. Leave the basil leaves on your altar overnight, and in the morning it will be ready for any magical work. Perform this ritual once a month to boost your altar's sacred powers.

Mindful observation

There's a lot to be said for a little meditation each day. Meditation allows us to be aware of ourselves in relation to the world around us – in other words, it encourages us to be mindful of the Earth and nature's magic.

As I touched on earlier, I find walking to be one of the best ways to meditate. While you walk, remember to be aware of and in tune with your surroundings. You may even want to take along a journal so that you can jot down any observations and sketch the beautiful scenery, or to take out your camera to snap a photo to capture the moment.

Notice the stones on the ground, the trees or the sea nearby. Listen to the waves, tune in to the sounds of birds, bees or the rustling of leaves. Smell the fragrances of nature, flowers, dung heaps, blossom, the earthy smells of damp trees, the ground itself, or the oceanic odours of the coast.

While you're walking, indulge in the beautiful feast before your eyes and take the opportunity to write a spell yourself. Reflect for a moment on how a universal energy – whether you want to call it *ch'i*, *prana*, or soul – permeates the Earth.

Respect nature, and nature respects you. Talk to the trees (see page 52), the plants, the fauna you meet on your way. Feel the energy around you and be intuitively aware of how it makes your senses react. Do you walk through a damp, dark glade and feel scared or uncomfortable? Out in the sunshine, do you feel relaxed and calm? What effect do nature's landscapes have on you, and why? What associations is your mind making? What has maybe influenced you to react this way?

If you can, take walks at different times of day in different landscapes. Early morning, midday (if it's not too hot), early evening, and dusk or dawn if possible, to experience the Earth and its relationship to the Sun; the way light falls at different times of day, shadow lengths, cool spots, hot spots, different energies.

Observing your reactions to all this will bring you closer to the magical nature of yourself as part of the Earth's energy.

Daily magic practice

Apart from communing with nature, here is a simple practice you can do at home to remind you of your natural magic powers.

You will need:

1 white candle
5 to 10 natural items (e.g. pebbles, shells, crystals, twigs, dried flowers or herbs)
jar with a lid

1. Light the candle and place your natural ingredients on a table or your sacred altar. One by one, place each item in the jar. As you

do so, repeat the charm: 'In this jar is magic made, for all of nature's world today.'

2. When you have finished filling the jar, leave it near a window so that it can absorb the light of the Sun.

3. Each day, open your jar, touch and stir your ingredients a little before refastening the lid. This way, you will be always in touch with the magic of the Earth, especially if you can't get out into a rural environment.

Clearing sacred spaces

It's important to remove negative energy from not only your home, but your garden and the sacred spaces you go to perform your Earth magic. By removing negativity from these areas, you will be more likely to achieve your intentions and goals. If, for example, you're surrounded by geopathic stress from bad psychic or electromagnetic energy, it will be harder to connect to beneficial energy. Geopathic stress is simply negative Earth energy, usually caused by the following sources.

Underground:

- water courses
- underground trains

- subsidence
- potholes
- earthquakes and geological fault lines
- plague pits (particularly in Europe where there were mass graves for victims of the bubonic plague)
- burial mounds
- disturbance by fauna and flora

Overhead:

- electrical powerlines
- large metal structures
- high-rise tower blocks
- satellites
- radar and all forms of unwanted electromagnetic energy

Here are some different methods to help you clear the negative energy and geopathic stress from your sacred spaces.

Smudging

Among many indigenous peoples worldwide, the burning of herbs or incense forms part of a ritual to cleanse and purify either oneself or the energy of a sacred place. This practice is commonly known as 'smudging'.

Smudging wands are simple to use and can be bought in most New Age stores worldwide, but it is even better if you can make your own. To do so, use either a bunch of twiggy herbs or plants that evoke the right atmosphere to cleanse, purify and align yourself to positive energy.

Use any or all of the following herbs for the best results:

Sage This is the most widely used type of smudging stick in magic. Driving out negativity, it purifies, cleanses and brings spiritual calm, positivity and stillness to the environment. White sage is favoured but common sage will do.

Lavender Often used for purifying and cleansing, lavender is also for psychic protection before casting difficult spells, as well as to enhance psychic awareness and create a sense of joyful peace.

Cedarwood This is a great smudging wand for removing all forms of negativity, and also to bring warmth, clarity, protection and tranquillity to a new home, sacred space or garden.

SMUDGING RITUAL

Making your own smudging sticks will engage you with a plant's magical qualities before you clear your sacred space.

You will need:

> bunch of fresh twigs or flowers (including one or
>   all of the herbs listed above)

a warm, dry place for drying your materials
length of twine or raffia
candle

1. Lay out your chosen flora in a straight line in a dry, warm place, and leave this to dry out for two weeks. Alternatively, you can tie one end of the bunch with twine and hang it up by a window or near your oven to accelerate the process, but be careful as the bunch will shrink as the stems dry out.

2. Once your chosen flora has dried out, make a slip knot using the twine and loop this around one end of your bunch. Now bind the twine round and round the bunch as tightly as you can. When you reach the end, go back over the bunch in the other direction so the twine makes a criss-cross effect. You now have your smudging wand.

3. When you are ready, take the smudging wand and light one end of it with a candle. Gently blow on the stick if you see flames – the aim is for it to smoke or smoulder.

4. Take your smudging wand and wave it around the place where you are going to perform magic. (You can also take your smudging stick with you as a cleansing and protective aid when you go out in rural environments.) As you do so, repeat the following phrase: 'With this wand all negative energy is removed, and I give thanks to all of nature for its protection, so mote it be.'

Candle safety

Always remember to place candles in secure hold-ers, away from any flammable materials or drapery. If you are using tea-light candles, put them on a saucer or in a tea-light holder – and never leave a lighted candle unattended.

DAILY PERSONAL PROTECTION RITUAL

You also need to protect yourself from all kinds of negative energy when you perform magic. So practise this simple ritual on a daily basis and make it just as much a part of your routine as taking a shower or brushing your hair.

Every morning, stand in a quiet place (whether in your home or outside) and raise your face skywards.

Stretch out your arms either side of you, and spread open your fingers. Now rhythmically move up and down just the little fingers of both hands as you say out loud, 'the fifth element protects me now', then do the same with the fourth (ring) finger of both hands, and say, 'the fourth element protects me now', then do the same with the third finger of both hands and say, 'the third element protects me now', then repeat with the second element finger and finally the thumb as first element. When you have finished, embrace your body by folding your arms across your chest, with your left hand on your right shoulder, your right hand on your left shoulder. Say, 'I am now protected by the power of the five elements.'

Energy dowsing

Another way you can engage with the energies of the Earth and get a better understanding of them is through a dowsing pendulum, which allows you to dowse for good and negative energy. As touched on earlier, negative energy often arises from geopathic stress, but it can also take the form of negative psychic energy, which, for example, can be left behind by the former occupants of a house, building or garden or even found out in the wild. This kind of stress is often caused by malevolent or unresolved conflicts and haunted places where tragedy has occurred.

Dowsing with a crystal pendulum to find good or negative energy will enable you to banish negativity or maximise positivity and create balance in the landscape. Dowsing is best known as an effective method for finding underground water courses, which you can do with willow dowsing rods. But its magical application for getting answers, decision-making or divination purposes has also been part of folk magic worldwide.

The dowsing pendulum
Dowsing pendulums have been used for thousands of years. The ancient Egyptians used water diviners and

dowsing pendulums to decide on the best places to grow crops, and in medieval Europe dowsing was frequently used for discovering ores, water courses and minerals and crystals.

So how does it work? Tiny involuntary movements of the hand holding the dowsing pendulum cause the crystal to move. Universal energy flows through you without your knowing it, and it is this energy that makes the muscles in your arm and hand react. This is called the 'ideomotor' response and the pendulum simply amplifies these minuscule movements.

To get started, choose a crystal pendulum that you really like, and check its weight feels heavy enough for you. The weight is important, and you'll find that heavier crystal pendulums are usually better as they allow for a greater swing. Shape is also important, as the best pendulums are shaped like pyramids, cylinders or equally faceted crystals such as diamonds.

The simplest way to hold a dowsing pendulum is to grip the top of the cord between your thumb and forefinger, with your arm held out from your elbow at waist level while you lean on a table. You will soon find it begins to move for you. However, before you set off to test the energy of your space with your pendulum, you need to know what the direction of each swing means.

How to check the swing of a dowsing pendulum

The pendulum can move in four possible directions: back and forth (towards your body and away from it), from side to side, clockwise or anticlockwise. Here is how to check what these mean.

1. Sit down at a table and lean your elbow on it, with the cord of the pendulum gripped between your finger and thumb. Keep your legs uncrossed and your body upright.
2. Ask a question to which you know the answer, for example, 'What is my name?' Then say your name.
3. The pendulum will eventually begin to move in one of the four directions described above. This direction is likely to be your 'yes' swing. To confirm whether this is your 'yes' swing, ask the pendulum another question where you know that the answer is yes.
4. To find out which direction is your 'no' swing, ask a silly question – where you know the answer is 'no', of course! Now the pendulum will swing in the opposite direction to your 'yes' swing. Again, check this is definitely a 'no' swing, with a follow-up question.

5. For 'don't know', you'll be left with two possible swings out of the four directions, so the easiest thing is to use both for a 'don't know' reply. In other words, and to make it easy, you will have three possible replies from the four possible directions of swing: one 'yes', one 'no' and two 'don't knows'.

Whenever you go to a new sacred place, stand in a quiet, reflective state, hold out your crystal pendulum and ask a simple question such as 'Is this a good place to cast a magic spell?' or 'Is there negative energy here?' If your pendulum doesn't respond with a yes or no, then it's worth moving a few meters away and trying again to see if the swing changes, as 'don't know' swings occur when geopathic energy – rather like a mobile phone signal – is weak or faint. When your pendulum indicates that you've found a good spot, cast your spell. If there is negative energy but you don't have an alternative space to perform your spell, use a smudging stick to dispel the negativity or perform the following ritual.

SPELL TO REMOVE NEGATIVITY IN OUTDOOR SPACES

Perform this simple spell if you encounter any form of negative energy when outside.

You will need:

cedarwood essential oil
1 white quartz crystal

1. Place your white quartz in front of you and drip five drops of the essential oil onto it as you repeat:

   *'With this work, all negativity be gone from
           this place.
   This circle gives me protection within the
           distance made.'*

2. Next, walk round the crystal in a clockwise direction to make a circle, before doing the same in an anticlockwise direction.
3. Now stand in the middle of your circle beside the crystal. You have removed any negativity from your sacred space and can work there with positive protection.

Visualisation and imagination

Both visualisation and imagination are often used when working with an incantation, spell or other magical practice. Activating your imagination and visualising ideas engages the intuitive right side of your brain, rather than the logical left side. By tuning in to your imagination and intuition, you will become more aware too of the powers of your own magical self.

Here are two very simple visualisation practices you can do at any time if you are new to visualising:

Watch a play Close your eyes and think of something you like doing, or someone you love. Try to see this visualisation as a play before your eyes (some say it's easier when your eyes are closed, but personally I find it easier with my eyes open and unfocused on anything before me!).

Imagine a blackboard Next, close (or not) your eyes and imagine a blackboard. Now see yourself writing words on the blackboard or letters or numbers. See your hand, see your words, repeat the words aloud as if you were reading them off the blackboard.

ROOT YOURSELF IN THE GREEN EARTH

If you've got the hang of creating mental pictures or movies in your head, do the following visualisation exercise to connect to the magic of the Earth.

1. Close your eyes and imagine that your feet have roots reaching down deep inside the Earth – just like a tree.
2. As you see these roots in your mind, imagine that the colour green is flowing deep within the

planet, spreading up through the Earth's crust. This colour of natural magic begins to slowly work its way up through your feet, and then into your legs, torso, arms, hands and head. Let it rise up through you slowly. See the colour filling you up until you are completely green, calm, relaxed and magical inside.

3. Now gradually imagine the green washing slowly away back down into the Earth and picture your roots in greenness forever. You are now connected to the magic of the Earth. If you ever feel lost, or disconnected to your magical power, repeat this visualisation.

Journaling

Having a lovely book that is precious and unique to you, filled with your wise words, ideas, thoughts and feelings, as well as sketches, poems, spells and other ingredients, is the key to the success of many a magic-maker's practice. In Wiccan magic, this kind of book is usually called a Book of Shadows and is like the mysterious grimoire I referred to in the Introduction.

You could also fill in entries like a diary, and record your practices or rituals on a daily basis. For example, how did it feel when you planted those first seeds? What happened when you saw the Full Moon; did your spell work?

You can also add pressed flowers or herbs to remind you

of certain times of the year or seasons when you revive or rework specific rituals. The more you write up your experiences, the more strongly you will feel a connection to the magic you are creating.

There is a belief that handwriting, drawing, sketching and calligraphy are a type of magical art in themselves, connecting our intuitive brain via the pen and paper to the power of the universe. So remember, the medium that you use to create your unique handwritten scrawl is far more empowering than any keyboard or modern form of technology.

The guardian witch's store cupboard

The spells in this book rely heavily on nature's bounty; from shells and crystals to flowers and herbs, you'll find that an array of natural ingredients is needed for rituals and enchantments.

Some of the most important things to get you started include:

- Crystals – white quartz, malachite, green tourmaline, red agate, obsidian, citrine and moonstone
- Essential oils – ylang-ylang, rose, cedarwood and mint
- A calendar of the phases of the Moon
- A list of Wiccan festivities and important dates for spell work

- And, of course, don't forget to keep precious foraged items such as shells, leaves, nuts or pressed flowers in your store cupboard too

Find a space to store away all of your precious treasures – this could be a cupboard in your kitchen or a shoebox under the bed, it's entirely up to you. Once you've selected the perfect space, make sure to use your smudging stick to cleanse it of any negative energy and to reinforce positivity.

Now you are a guardian witch . . .

Now that you are beginning to embrace your role as a guardian witch, you need to remember to take care of yourself as well as the well-being of Mother Earth. What are your intentions for yourself and the planet?

1. Ask yourself the following questions and answer them honestly:

- Do I sincerely care about the future of our planet?
- Do I care about myself and where I fit in here on Earth?
- Do I deserve love just by virtue of being here on Earth?

- Do I truly want to give goodness to the planet and create a better place for myself and for all?
- What are my intentions?

2. Write down your answers in your journal or Book of Shadows to remind you of these motives every time you engage in your work.

If you have answered the questions about your intention truthfully, you will feel the magic begin to grow within your soul, heart, spirit, mind and body, as if you have sown seeds within your inner sacred garden. Now it's time to create a replica garden in the outside world.

Chapter 6

The Sacred Garden

The word 'sacred' implies the embodiment of something spiritual or a revered belief, and it also means that the place, thing or object is cherished by the gods as well. The earliest sacred gardens were not cultivated as such. In ancient Mesopotamia and Greece, sacred gardens were rural places such as groves and areas of land beside springs and rivers that were believed to be inhabited by gods, nymphs or other spirits. Trees, fruit, plants and flowers were associated with particular deities, such as the oak with Zeus, the laurel with Apollo and the myrtle with Aphrodite.

One of the best known mythological sacred gardens was the Garden of the Hesperides. This was the apple orchard given to Hera by Gaia, when Hera agreed to marry the reckless god of the heavens, Zeus. Each tree in the grove bore golden apples that offered the gift of immortality. The nymphs who tended the garden were known as the Hesperides, but they began stealing the fruit for themselves, so Hera employed a fierce dragon to guard the apples.

However, Eris, the goddess of discord, still managed to enter the garden and pluck an apple from a tree. She inscribed it 'to the fairest' and rolled it into the wedding feast of the sea nymph Thetis and the mortal Peleus, to which she was not invited. She hoped to create jealousy between Hera, Aphrodite and Athena, and her act ultimately led to the Trojan War.

Gaia's gift of the apple orchard is a great metaphor for how Mother Nature has provided us with all we need, yet we may still be taking more than we perhaps have a right to. Before we anger the goddesses further, perhaps we can tend our own gardens and look after the world a little better, to show our belief and respect?

Sacred gardens are filled with archetypal symbols in their flowers, their designs, their myth, and their magical associations with nature's spirits and deities. Create a sacred garden and you create a magical environment for yourself, too.

Your sacred garden

Your sacred garden will become the most delightful place on Earth, because it is your creation and a physical embodiment of both your inner sanctuary and of your deepest magical self which exists right on your doorstep. It doesn't have to be huge or complicated, but when your spirit and soul are invested in this environment, you will show the world that you care and that you are connected to it.

Your sacred garden is also a symbol of the Earth. It has its own geography, topology and regions. It is your own unique landscape that is sacrosanct to you and the planet. In this chapter, we are going to look at how to create this garden, where to locate it, how to protect it from negative energy, and the basic positive attributes you need to incorporate in it to ensure it is a beneficial place in which to plant your desires and dreams. It also a place where you can work your magic for the Earth's well-being too.

How to create a sacred garden

The plot and size of your sacred garden depends on your available outdoor space, but also think about how it can be incorporated into the rest of your surroundings. You may only have a narrow balcony or five whole acres, but the beauty of a sacred garden is that it's an incredibly personal space however large it is, so do what feels right for you.

Design

One thing to bear in mind when mapping out your garden is the form it takes. A spiral garden conforms to the symbolic energy of creativity and growth. However, if you prefer a geometric design of squares, say, or a circle sliced into twelve equal planting areas (as per the signs of the zodiac) or anything else you fancy, then that is more important than sticking to a rulebook.

You can plant anything you like, but a simple sacred garden might consist only of lavender, herbs and a mixture of wildflowers to attract bees and other pollinators. What you plant, of course, depends on your local ecosystem, terrain, weather and environment.

Take your time to think about where you will plant things, where you will sit or meditate, and the best compass directions and positions for good growth. Ask yourself where the Sun will be at midday. Do you have a south-facing or north-facing aspect? Which plants can be grown successfully in a heavily shaded garden or one that has very little Sun in winter, and so on? Plot your plot, design your design, and always remember the true purpose behind your sacred garden.

The perfect indoor garden

Don't worry if you don't have an outdoor space. There are lots of alternatives that will offer the same healing benefits. Here are just a few for you to consider:

Use a window box Fill a window box with your favourite plants, annuals or perennials – and make sure to enjoy, cultivate and nurture your chosen plants. Herbs such as mint (although invasive), parsley and rosemary are perfect all-round botanicals that can be used both in the kitchen and for spellwork.

Cultivate a plant pot The same goes for a solitary plant pot if you lack space. Fill the pot with wildflower seeds or miniature and low-growing herbs like thyme or marjoram.

Display an artwork If you are struggling for space, then another option is to get creative. Paint, sketch or make a collage of a fabulous sacred garden of your imagining, or find a photograph or painting that you particularly admire and connect with, and hang it on the south-facing wall of your most used room. This will help to maximise positive energy.

What to cultivate in your garden

Gardens are usually filled with plants, stones and water features – not forgetting fascinating structural plants or trees that give a garden shape, balance and dynamic energy. But you can also incorporate other magical accessories, such as a small sheltered altar for crystal magic, or even a swing, a hammock or an area to meditate and relax in. If you have enough space, you can create a shelter where you can light candles to perform rituals, or build a raised bed of stones that can be used to petition your favourite deities by placing a ring of flower petals or an empowerment crystal there during certain lunar cycles.

Of course, if you don't have the space for a garden, and only a plant pot on a kitchen windowsill, then improvisation can be magical and fun too. For a plant-pot sacred garden, imagine everything in miniature. Plant a favourite herb or annual flower to represent your current needs or desires. Perhaps lay a circle of crystals around it, and when appropriate light candles to enhance specific lunar phases. Care for your plant as you would a bigger garden. Talk to it, walk your mind through the stems and petals, touch the soil, sprinkle a few drops of water on the leaves like garden rain, or pluck a leaf or petal and hold it close to you when you meditate or begin spellwork. Water it when necessary and as you do so tell your plant how sacred it is and give thanks for its presence.

What is a sacred garden for?

Now that you've created your sacred garden, what should you be using it for? It's a place which you can use to meditate, connect to nature and perform your spells. Be kind to this space and care for it by growing, cultivating and respecting its unique magic. Here are some more suggestions for ways to enjoy your sacred garden:

Growing healing and culinary plants
You can grow herbs and many other botanicals to harvest to use for their specific qualities. You can

grow lesser-known medicinal herbs such as comfrey or feverfew, well-known culinary ones such as parsley and thyme, or mint and nettles to make a tonic or tea. There are also a wide variety of plants known for their spiritual and emotional healing powers, such as lavender (a must-have in any sacred garden) for calm and protection, lilies for spiritual awakening and roses for loving relationships. By growing these plants you are creating a bond with the Earth, and making it clear that they are sacred to you.

Worshipping to connect to a specific spiritual goal

Many plants are associated with nature deities, spirits, crystals and four of the five elements. You may want to be more in tune with your psychic abilities, for example; in which case, creating a small pond or water feature in your garden would help to enhance all aspects of your intuitive power and a sense of oneness with the universe. You may want to worship and be blessed by the presence of deities such as Gaia, the horned fertility god, Cernunnos, or the vegetation god, the Green Man. For acts of worship, you can place a statue in the middle of your garden or create a shrine where you leave offerings to the spirit or deity of your choice.

Basking in the joy of being

Your sacred garden may be more of a place to relax, to enjoy, to roll out your yoga mat, or to meditate and reach up your arms to the Sun. Whatever makes you feel joyful, content, zen-like or even fit and healthy (you may even use this space to work out or to work on your novel or painting) can be incorporated and organised accordingly, with seating, outdoor furniture or water features; plants which are heavily scented at night or shading and cooling on a hot summer's day.

Amplifying your connection to your inner spiritual garden

Your sacred garden will immediately enhance your alignment with nature and make you feel that you are growing, nurturing and promoting you own inner spiritual sanctuary just as much as the physical garden you are tending. Surrounded by nature, you will bloom as your flowers blossom; you will grow as your wildflowers spring to life and you will be aware of all your senses as you tend, dig, prune, harvest, sow or water your garden, enhancing the creative spirit of yourself.

Expressing gratitude

Your sacred garden is, most of all, a place to give thanks to Mother Earth, so it's important to incorporate some form of shrine, be it a water feature, a standing stone or a pile of stones, where you can leave regular offerings. These offerings may be anything you choose: seeds, flowers, a folded secret note in a jar, a poem or incantation, or simply a stone. If you are working with a plant-pot garden, simply leave your petition beside the pot to show your thanks.

Geomancy

Your home and garden are sacred, a place where you live, laugh, sleep, reflect on past events and make plans for your future. So you need to protect and nurture it too. An old form of divination known as geomancy, translated from ancient Greek meaning 'foresight by Earth', is the way to harmoniously align the energies of your immediate environment to improve your overall well-being. Geomancy originated in ancient Persia, where shamans drew mysterious patterns in the sand to connect to Earth spirits. Later, in medieval Europe, the famous magician and astrologer Cornelius Agrippa developed mystical symbols from these ancient shamanic patterns. Today, geomancy continues to offer a magical way to harness protective energy in the environment.

Using simple grid systems and patterns that incorporate crystals, you can work with geomancy to align your home, your garden and yourself to the positive energies of the Earth. These magical grid patterns can be used to activate anything – from healing, love and career progress to prosperity and protection. You can also use the grids to eliminate psychic negative energy in your surroundings, whether out in the countryside or in your home. Whether you have only a handful of stones, a few polished gems, or a pouch of quartz, you can enhance and channel the power of the universe through the placement of stones and protect your home from geopathic stress and negative energy. By engaging with the soil itself when you place crystals on or in the ground, you are showing your respect for nature too.

The rituals below suggest the best possible crystal to use for each desired outcome. However, if you do not have any of these to hand, you can use pebbles or stones as a substitute. Just make sure you use the right number of stones and place them in the correct grid pattern for the magic to work.

RITUAL FOR A SUCCESSFUL RESOLUTION TO A PROBLEM

Shungite is a crystal that encourages help from others and the successful resolutions to transient problems.

You will need:

6 pieces of shungite
pen or pencil and paper (optional)

1. Mark out a spiral pattern in your sacred garden. If that's not possible, any outdoor space will do, or you can even sketch a spiral on a piece of paper.
2. Place the six pieces of shungite clockwise along the spiral, taking care to ensure that they're evenly spaced out. If you're outside, walk slowly around the spiral six times and repeat six times: 'This [the problem] is resolved by the presence of beneficial outside influences.' If you've chosen to use paper,

repeat the same process but trace the spiral with your finger instead.

3. Leave the grid pattern to work its magic for six days, then remove the stones and you will see results.

RITUAL FOR THE PROTECTION OF LOVED ONES

Moonstone is a crystal known for its nurturing, healing and protective properties. This moonstone ritual is particularly aimed at protecting family members and others close to you. The ritual works best outdoors, as you'll need to leave your grid in the moonlight to capture the natural nurturing power of the Moon.

You will need:

7 pieces of moonstone

1. When there is a Waxing or New Crescent Moon, lay out the pieces of moonstone in the shape of a five-pointed star. The first moonstone goes in the centre, with five further equidistant pieces mapping out the star around it. Keep the last moonstone in your pocket.

2. Leave this formation in place for one lunar cycle to empower your family or loved ones with protective energy, and carry the seventh moonstone with

you during the day and keep it under your pillow at night. After one lunar cycle, remove all stones and keep in a cherished place.

RITUAL FOR FINANCIAL STABILITY

Amethyst is the stone of integrity, reliability, truth and justice.

You will need:

pen or pencil and paper
6 small pieces of amethyst
6 large stones

1. On a piece of paper, draw your Sun sign (also known as your star sign) symbol. Then take your pieces of amethyst and wrap them in the piece of paper, making sure that the symbol you've drawn is on the inside.

2. Find a suitable outdoor space and dig a shallow bed, before carefully placing your wrapped amethyst pieces in it. Cover your package with soil and once this is done, place a large stone next to it.

3. Every time you pass by or visit the site, place a new stone until you have a circle of six stones around the amethyst bed. On your seventh visit, simply dig up and remove the amethyst pieces in the paper – leaving the stones in a circle – and

store the crystals in a safe place. You will soon be rewarded with financial, material or family stability.

RITUAL FOR CLARITY ON FUTURE GOALS

Azurite is the crystal of clarity and truth.

You will need:

4 pieces of azurite
compass (e.g. on your phone)

1. Take four pieces of azurite and put them in a special place. (This might be your sacred garden or any outdoor space that is significant to you.) Align them to the four compass points, with each piece set about one metre (three feet) apart.
2. First, stand at the east-facing crystal and, while looking in an easterly direction, affirm: 'My goals are favourable, my gain is for me, but I give thanks for all that I receive and will return it with love.'
3. Move to the south-facing crystal, look in a southerly direction and affirm: 'Truth and clarity are necessary to see my way forward.'
4. Move to the west-facing crystal, look in a westerly direction and affirm: 'I now know what my true goals are and will attain them.'
5. Finally, move to the north-facing crystal, look in

a northerly direction and affirm: 'Thank you, the four directions, for bringing me the truth. I will follow the pathway.'

6. Leave the crystals in place for one lunar cycle, and you will be blessed with insight about your future.

RITUAL FOR FREEDOM FROM THE PAST

Obsidian represents living in the present, stability and acceptance. This ritual can be used to free yourself from the past and find stability in yourself.

You will need:

7 pieces of obsidian

1. Place six pieces of obsidian in a circle in your sacred garden or an outside space where they won't be disturbed. Place the seventh piece in the centre, and repeat:

   'With obsidian here, the past be gone
   And present and future be as one;
   My inner self has no regret
   And all that's been, has gone to rest.'

2. Leave the grid in place for two Full Moon cycles, then remove and keep your crystals stored in a safe place.

RITUAL FOR KICK-STARTING PROJECTS OR IDEAS

Blue lace agate is for clarity, confidence and conviction.

You will need:

3 pieces of blue lace agate

1. To make sure you can get projects off the ground, speak with conviction or communicate your needs successfully, place three pieces of blue lace agate in the form of a triangle in the western part of your sacred garden or outdoor space, with the top of the triangle pointing west.
2. Each day, for three days, move all of the stones one place further on, until they've all been placed at each point of the triangle once.
3. On the fourth day, remove the stones and put them in a pouch or box to keep in your desk or workspace. Your plans should now come to fruition.

RITUAL FOR RESILIENCE IN SEEING THINGS THROUGH

Bloodstones promote courage and strength, and can help you to achieve great results by staying true to yourself.

You will need:

8 pieces of bloodstone
length of ribbon, twine or raffia

1. When there is a Waxing Moon, place the eight bloodstones in two horizontal parallel lines of four stones each in your sacred garden or an outside place that won't be disturbed.
2. Circle the two parallel lines with your piece of ribbon, twine or raffia to contain the energy. Stand before the circle and say, 'I am guided by my inner strength and am determined to achieve what I set out to do. I believe only in myself and trust my instincts.'
3. Leave the stones untouched until the Full Moon, then remove all but one from the circle. The last bloodstone will need to stay in place until the New Crescent Moon; then you may remove it and you can achieve all you set out to do.

RITUAL FOR PROSPERITY AND HOME PROTECTION

Citrine is the stone of prosperity, both materially and also of the mind, soul and spirit. This ritual will also promote protection for your home and family.

You will need:

pen or pencil and paper
5 pieces of citrine

1. During a Waxing Moon phase, take a piece of paper and draw a spiral (as big or small as you like) in an anticlockwise direction, and then draw a circle around it to contain its energy. Place the paper on a table near a window or in a sheltered space in your sacred garden to capture the Moon's positive energy.
2. Next, place the five pieces of citrine equidistant along the spiral pathway. As you do so, repeat the following words:

    'With five citrine I cast this spell
    To bring good wealth to keep me well.'

3. Leave until the night of the Full Moon, then remove the citrine and keep in a safe place. Fold the talisman five times, and finally write on the last folded side: 'Wealth and happiness to all.'
4. Seal your intention by burying the paper in your sacred garden, or even in your recycling bin.

PART THREE

Earth Connection Rituals

By establishing a strong bond and a symbiotic relationship with Mother Earth, you will create vitalising energy that will mutually benefit both you and the planet. This section of the book offers a wide range of rituals and practices to enable you to connect to nature and bring well-being into your life while giving goodness back to the planet at the same time. As chapter 7 explains in more depth, you will find that the rituals come in pairs, to help you give back to nature as much as you receive from it.

Aligning with nature's energies will enable you to call on Earth magic whenever you are out in the countryside. And even in an urban environment you will find it easier to recall and instantly connect to nature's magic, and in doing so invest in the well-being of the Earth.

As mentioned in the Introduction, the ingredients used in these spells and charms draw upon the most ancient, traditional or best-loved correspondences related to magic work. Naturally, as you progress with your own natural magic, you can find new ingredients and other correspondences that may be more suited to your personal location. (See Glossary of Correspondences.)

Chapter 7

Flora and Botanicals

In this chapter, we are going to connect closely with the world of plants, flowers, herbs and trees. You will discover the pleasures of the senses – perhaps a realisation that you can communicate with the rose; an awareness that as you pluck a ripe blackberry you will be rewarded with its taste; that when you see a field of poppies or a distant forest, it will be a feast for the soul as well as the eyes.

To prepare for this work and these connections with

the natural world, we are first going to look at a practice to help bring in positive energy.

How to inspirit positive energy

The word 'inspirit' means to encourage and allow others to feel truly alive. Here, I will be using the term to refer to the act of energising the life force or spirit within all living things. In carrying out the practices in this chapter, you will promote goodwill not only for yourself but for the planet. You will encourage and inspire Mother Earth with your best intentions and show that you are as much a part of nature as nature is a part of you.

There are two parts to all of the rituals in the next five chapters: the first part will help you to connect directly to nature so you no longer feel separate from it and can thus discover your magical alliance with Mother Earth; while the second part will allow you to maintain the balance of Earth's energy and inspirit the Earth with goodness too. To ensure the success of your magical connection to nature, perform as many of the rituals as you can from the following section – and remember that it's essential to do both parts of them. If we take for ourselves, we must also return something of ourselves.

Let's get started with a lovely practice that will help us to engage consciously with nature . . .

Crystal engagement ritual

To engage with nature we must invest in it, so take your time when choosing and buying the following five crystals, which correspond to the five categories in nature and will become your friends for life.

You will need:

1 citrine (for sky and stars)
1 moonstone (for sacred places)
1 red agate (for the landscape)
1 green tourmaline (for fauna
    and flora)
1 white quartz crystal (for the spirit
    of you)
pouch in which to store your crystals

1. Place your five crystals in your pouch and find a quiet, private place outdoors.
2. Take out the crystals one at a time, in no particular order, and make a circle, with the first crystal to the north, and placing the remaining four in a clockwise direction.
3. Make clear your intention by saying or thinking:

'These gifts of nature are mine to share,
To bring harmonious joy to all that's here.'

4. Now take up each crystal in turn and hold it in your hand while repeating:

   'With nature's magic I become one with all,
   and all is one.'

5. Return your crystals to your pouch. You can use this ritual to reinforce your powers whenever you feel you are lacking that inner connection with nature.

Now you are ready to practise the following rituals to align to the magic of the Earth. Please remember to perform the second part as well as the first.

Oak

Magic tradition: Celtic, Norse, Roman and Druid
Sacred meaning: security, perseverance, strength and endurance

With over four hundred varieties, the fabulous oak has been used for thousands of years to make everything from buildings to wine barrels and cork. The oak was sacred to the Greek god Zeus, so much so that his oracle at Dodona centred on an ancient oak tree where priestesses would use the rustling of the oak's leaves to divine the future. Norse myths tell of how the oak was a powerful stabilising force and was associated mostly with deities who controlled thunder, lightning, and storms. In Celtic folklore, oak twigs were tied into a cross and hung up in the home for protection against negativity.

RITUAL TO CONNECT WITH THE DURABLE POWER OF OAK

In this ritual, the properties of hematite combine with the durability of oak to enhance your personal integrity and well-being.

You will need:

3 foraged oak leaves (or 3 cut-out images of leaves)
3 pieces of hematite

1. Place the three oak leaves in a triangle shape in your sacred garden, or inside in a safe place where they won't be disturbed. Now repeat the following charm:

   *'Now hear the leaves rustling among
        the trees:
   The first augurs strength, aligns my
        bended knees,*

The second to empower me with the whispers
of the oak,
The last to surround me, its protection
now invoked.'

2. Lay one piece of hematite on each leaf, repeat the charm and leave in place overnight. In the morning, remove the leaves and hematite and you will be empowered with the oak tree's strength of purpose.

OAK RITUAL OF THANKS

1. Please go out and hug an oak tree at midday (when solar energy is at its strongest) if you can. As you do so, turn your gaze up to the rustling leaves and watch the light glinting through the branches. Focus on exchanging mutual well-being, as if you were embracing a friend.

2. To generate a deep-rooted sense of unity, repeat the following words: 'Blessings to the power of the Spirit of the Oak for giving me positive strength, which I return with integrity for all.'

3. Don't worry if you can't get out and hug a real tree – you can always make an oak tree mood board. Simply stick or pin oak-tree imagery all over a pin-board, add real or fake oak leaves, acorns or twigs, place in the centre of your home and repeat the above affirmation.

Lavender

Magic tradition: Europe, Asia and Wicca
Sacred meaning: protection, calm seduction and a positive spirit

An aromatic member of the *Lamiaceae* family, lavender is native to the Mediterranean and is cultivated in many temperate well-drained terrains worldwide. In ancient Egypt and Persia, it was used to heal and cleanse wounds. According to legend, Cleopatra used lavender oil to seduce suitors in her power games, while the asp that poisoned her was thought to have hidden among her very own lavender bushes. Lavender was added to water in ancient Christian purification rituals, while medieval monasteries later cultivated lavender in their physic gardens for its healing powers. In European folk customs, lavender was placed under a lover's pillow to induce romantic thoughts; once married a couple would place lavender under the mattress to ensure marital passion. Dried lavender is still commonly used in pillows to induce a good night's sleep and pleasant dreams.

RITUAL FOR AWAKENING TO THE HEALING POWER OF LAVENDER

Awakening to the healing power of lavender helps improve the mind, protect, heal and encourages fertility and calm.

You will need:

a handful of fresh or dried lavender
5 drops of lavender water, essence or essential oil

1. Hold your lavender in your non-writing hand and, with the other, drip the water, oil or essence slowly onto the bunch as you say:

   'With lavender blue, its essence so true,
   I connect to the power of this herbal brew.
   Awaken my power, this healing be mine
   And all that is blessed, I know it be fine.'

2. Take up the bunch of lavender and breathe in the fragrance as you press your nose deeply into the flowers. Imagine you are a bee or a butterfly; how you will carry its power to your home, as you bathe in, soak up or awaken to its empowering qualities.

3. Leave the lavender under your pillow for one night, and then hang it upside down by a window for one lunar cycle to imbue you and your home with healing energy. You have now awakened that power deep within you too.

LAVENDER RITUAL OF THANKS

The best time to perform this ritual of thanks is when the lavender is in bud or flower.

You will need:

5 stems of lavender or an image of lavender bushes
1 small bottle of lavender essential oil
1 white candle (if using an image of lavender)

1. Take your lavender oil and anoint the five lavender flowers or buds, five being the magical number of Earth magic. If you are using an image, anoint it with five drops of the oil and then place the image beneath the lit white candle.
2. Repeat the following affirmation as you cup the stems in your hands or gaze at your image: 'I give my healing spirit back to herbs of love and protection in all things, and join all of nature with my magic words.'
3. Bow your head in thanks to the lavender and your positive spirit will be returned to the botanical world.

Dandelion

Magic tradition: Celtic, Wicca and European
Sacred meaning: solar power, wish-fulfilment and release

The name 'dandelion' derives from the French phrase *dent de lion*, which refers to the tooth-like edges of the leaves, and the lion, who in medieval imagery was often represented by the Sun with sharply pointed solar rays. This well-known healing plant has been used medicinally since ancient Greece. Not only is it a potent diuretic (hence its French name *pissenlit*, meaning urinating in bed), it is also a good source of vitamins A, C and K. Today, the leaves and the boiled roots are still often eaten in salads. Its beautiful seed head has given it local English names such as 'fortune-teller' and 'one o'clock'. These refer to traditional games in which the downy seed head is blown and the number of puffs it takes to blow away all the seeds are believed to tell the time of day or your fortune. We will be combining the power of the dandelion with that of the nettle in a two-fold magical practice (see below) that was once an ancient rite used by Celtic diviners.

Stinging nettle

Magic tradition: worldwide
Sacred meaning: protection, fertility, revival of spirit

Botanically known as *Urtica dioica*, the English word 'nettle' is derived from the Anglo-Saxon *noedl*, meaning needle. The Latin *Urtica* comes from *urendo*, burning. The stinging nettle was thought to have been brought to Great Britain by the invading Romans, who rubbed the burning leaves on their limbs to warm their blood. The nettle also has a cure for the sting within itself – its own juice. However, it's rare not to find a clump of nettles without its accompanying antidote, the dock leaf, growing nearby. Nettle leaves make a wonderful tonic either taken as a tea or soup, but must always be boiled before eating. In European magic traditions, nettles were burned to drive out negativity or unwanted spirits, or ground into a powder and used in spells to break curses.

ONE O'CLOCK ENCHANTMENT RITUAL

When you combine nettles with dandelion, you will discover a close connection to the healing and divination powers of nature. This ritual will enhance your connection to nature's healing energy. But do note that it is important to carry out this practice on a windless day.

You will need:

> a large handful of crushed nettle leaves (take care not to get stung if foraging), or five nettle teabags
> muslin pouch
> dandelions
> 1 green candle (optional)

1. Place your nettle leaves or teabags inside your muslin pouch.
2. Now pick an outdoor space, be it your garden, a park or anywhere you will be sure to encounter

dandelions. Look for a full dandelion seed head that has yet to be blown away by the wind, but do not attempt to pick it or disturb it.

3. Bend down, kneel or sit carefully beside the dandelion and place your pouch of nettles alongside the plant. Repeat in your head or whisper the following incantation before you begin:

'One o'clock, two o'clock, three o'clock, four
Binding nettles about my door;
Wind-borne blown this tisane be
Of burning pins and pissenlit.'

4. Now begin to blow on the seeds. As you blow, count how many times it takes to remove all the seeds. (Below you can find a fortune-telling correspondence used in folklore that will tell you your fortune for the day.) Whatever number of blows it takes will mark the best hour of day to drink and sip your nettle tea, which you can brew using the crushed nettle leaves or teabags; so if it took you five blows, then you should make and drink your tea at five o'clock. As you sip your tea, be sure to repeat the charm. If you do not like the taste of nettle tea, you can sprinkle the crushed nettle leaves onto a lit green candle to represent your sipping.

Dandelion seed head oracle

The number of puffs it takes to blow away all the dandelion seeds traditionally means the following:

One for progress
Two for relationship success
Three for a useful message
Four for utter fidelity
Five for creative enterprise
Six for domestic bliss
Seven for positive influences
Eight for riches
Nine for travel
Ten for fulfilment

DANDELION AND NETTLE RITUAL OF THANKS

This is a lovely ritual to express thanks for things happening as they should according to nature's cycles. This spell will return positive healing energy to nature and remind you that you can draw on nature's healing powers too. Perform it when you are in a relaxed, meditational state.

1. For this ritual, you will need to imagine that you are wandering through a garden where you have accidentally fallen into a bed of nettles. Try to feel

the stinging, burning pain and visualise the wheals forming across your body.

2. As you focus on these sensations, you remember that there are dock leaves growing nearby. Pluck the leaves and rub them on your skin to soothe the pain instantly.

3. Imagine next that you stumble across a bed of dandelions that have gone to seed. Bend down and pluck a dandelion seed head. Imagine blowing those seeds into the landscape as a symbolic blessing for nature. Isn't it remarkable how nature provided you with a painful moment, offered you a healing remedy and in return you are offering your own remedy?

Pomegranate

Magic tradition: ancient Greek, Judaism, Buddhism
Sacred meaning: well-being, abundance, fertility

The pomegranate was a symbol of the cycles of nature in ancient Greek mythology (see the myth of Persephone, page 11), and some biblical scholars believe that the pomegranate was also the forbidden fruit found in the Garden of Eden. In Judaism, the fruit is highly revered as it is said to have 613 seeds, which corresponds to the 613 commandments of the Torah. During Rosh Hashanah, the Jewish New Year, one seed is eaten at a time for good luck. In Buddhism, pomegranates, peaches and lemons are considered the three blessed fruits, as they are believed to drive away evil thoughts. In the European Middle Ages, the resemblance between a pomegranate and an imperial crown made it a symbol of power. In many magic traditions, pomegranates are the main ingredient of love potions.

POMEGRANATE RITUAL TO ALIGN TO THE CYCLES OF NATURE

The use of pomegranate in this ritual reminds us of both the myth of Persephone and our own connection to the natural rhythms of the Earth and the rewards of living in harmony with these.

You will need:

> 1 red candle
> 5 pomegranates
> shallow bowl
> basket, bag or box
> cling film or beeswax wraps

1. Light the red candle to invoke positive energy. Then cut open your five pomegranates, separate the seeds from the surrounding white pith and scrape them into the bowl. Once you are ready, place the bowl in front of the red candle.
2. Now repeat:

> *'With seeded jewels be my delight*
> *To know the seasons, day and night.'*

3. Wrap up the bowl of seeds, place it into your basket, bag or box, and blow out the candle. Take the seeds to an outdoor space where you can plant them safely in secret. If a suitable space doesn't come to mind, you can always do this at home using a planter and soil. Location isn't important; it's the act of returning the seeds to the Earth that will ensure you connect to the cycles of nature.

4. As you plant the seeds repeat the following charm:

   'With seeded jewels be my delight,
   I know the seasons, day and night.'

5. Return to the spot after one lunar cycle and repeat the incantation to maximise its goodwill benefits.

POMEGRANATE RITUAL OF THANKS

Spring and summer are the best times to perform this simple ritual to re-inspire your sense of growth and connection to nature.

You will need:

a few pomegranate seeds
flower pot

1. Remove the fleshy arils from the seeds. The aril is the shiny, juicy coating that makes each seed look like a jewel and gives the fruit its lush interior.

2. Plant a few pomegranate seeds in a pot about 3cm (1in) deep.

3. Keep the pot in a warm room for about thirty to forty days to allow the seeds to germinate. You can transfer the seedlings to individual pots once they have sprouted.

4. Bear in mind it can take a few years for a pomegranate tree to bear fruit – and it may not be exactly the fruit you expect to appear, due to the many cultivars available – but the flowers will be spectacular and worthy of your time and patience.

Basil

Magic tradition: Hindu, Buddhism and European
Sacred meaning: protection, fidelity and healing

Basil is one of the most revered herbs in folk magic, as well as being known for its incredible flavour. Originally indigenous to Asia, and a sacred plant in Hindu tradition, it is now cultivated throughout the world. Its European name derives from the Latin *basillicum* and Greek *basilikon*, meaning king. Its name also means that the herb has long been associated with the mythical Roman serpent known as the basilisk. In fact, the herb is thought to be the antidote for its venom. Basil was hung over doorways at medieval banquets as it was believed to calm all who entered, and, similarly, it will protect your home from unwanted intruders. Believed to promote fertility, fidelity, prosperity, wealth, abundance and inspiration, it was thought to be a healing balm for lost love. This was alluded to in the fourteenth-century Italian author Boccaccio's tales of love, collectively known as *The Decameron*, one of which was adapted by Keats in his poem *Isabella, or the Pot of Basil* (1818). The poem tells the story of Isabella, who falls in love with 'the wrong man', ultimately leading to his murder. Discovering his body, she buries his head in a pot of basil which she constantly nurtures to comfort herself and his soul.

RITUAL TO INVOKE BASIL'S POSITIVE HEALING ENERGY

While you're not about to bury anyone in a pot of basil in this ritual, you are going to bury a crystal!

You will need:

1 pot of basil
1 small piece of green tourmaline

1. Place your pot of basil in a sunny position and make sure to water it as needed.

2. Before you start picking the leaves to eat, bury your green tourmaline into the plant's moist soil. You don't want to dig too far – just enough so the tourmaline is hidden.

3. Leave the tourmaline in place while you enjoy the leaves of this flavoursome plant, removing the leaves from the top first to allow for new leaves to come through. If you see any flowers beginning to blossom, you want to nip them out straight away or your plant will die.

4. After one lunar cycle, remove the tourmaline, wash it and then place it on a sunny window ledge. You will soon benefit from the empowering energy it has drawn from the pot of basil.

BASIL RITUAL OF THANKS

To help balance the cycle of nature by giving back as much as you receive, perform this ritual at night under a Full Moon.

You will need:

1 basil plant

1. Pluck five basil leaves from your plant and place them in a moonlit spot to draw down the lunar energy and also to offer as a symbol of your fidelity to the universe.

2. In the morning, take your leaves to a natural body of water – if this isn't possible, a jar of spring or mineral water will do the trick – and shred them into the water to enhance your connection to nature.

Chapter 8

Fauna

The practices, rituals and spells in this chapter will help you to connect to the animal kingdom and to absorb and generate loving and healing energy to all living beings in the world around you. If necessary, repeat the crystal engagement ritual on page 97 as part of your preparations. And when working with the practices in this chapter, remember to perform the second ritual as well as the first, so that you give back to nature as well as take from it.

Red Admiral butterfly

Magic tradition: worldwide
Sacred meaning: change, transition, journey of the soul and rebirth

The butterfly is a symbol of transformation, which reflects its extraordinary life cycle – changing from chrysalis to caterpillar to winged beauty. The Red Admiral, indigenous to parts of North Africa, Europe, the Americas, Caribbean islands and Asia, migrates to the Northern Hemisphere in the warmth of the summer, where it lays its eggs on the common stinging nettle (see page 104). In ancient Greek mythology, the butterfly was seen as a symbol of the soul and personified as Psyche, the lover of Eros. In Asian cultures, butterflies represent happiness, and they are also a symbol of rebirth and joy to many indigenous peoples of the Americas. In Earth magic, the butterfly is seen as a welcome guest who may come and sit on your shoulder when you least expect her and bring you goodwill.

RITUAL TO ACCEPT AND MAKE SACRED THE CYCLES OF LIFE

The Red Admiral, as one of the most common butterflies worldwide, will enable you to connect to sacred cycles and to understand such transitions within yourself. In this ritual, agate represents the butterfly's symbolism of transformation, while citrine represents the butterfly's symbolism of flight.

You will need:

1 piece of red agate
1 piece of citrine
1 cut-out image of a Red Admiral
1 cardboard box

1. Place the crystals and the image in the cardboard box and venture out into a wooded area where you are likely to find nettles growing. If this isn't possible, don't worry. Instead settle into a sacred space and imagine that you're in a grove or a forest. Visualise that you are surrounded clumps of nettles and wildflowers, as rays of Sun shine through the trees above.

2. Find a comfortable place to sit where you can turn your head to the sky or the tree canopy and say:

   'For now the butterfly leaves my soul,
   Returns to bring lives new for old,
   With agate red and citrine hue
   I walk on down the path of truth.'

3. Hide the box in the woods perhaps near to the nettles, which are the Red Admiral's favourite breeding site. (But don't get stung in the process!)

4. Leave the box for one lunar cycle, and then return

to collect your box — now blessed with the butterfly's wings of happy change. Whenever you feel in need of a boost of happiness, take out the two crystals and hold them close to you.

RED ADMIRAL RITUAL OF THANKS

The best time to perform this ritual is in early to midsummer when the Red Admiral appears.

1. If you are lucky enough to live near a Red Admiral butterfly habitat, linger a while and observe one or more of these winging, capricious creatures as they go about their work. They, like you, are gardening this Earth, doing what the essence of being a butterfly impels them to do.

2. You may have to wait a while, but as soon as you see your first butterfly of the day, repeat the following charm to invoke the spirit of positive transformation:

My butterfly friend lives days of love
Of change, of joy, of hopes above;
With blessings free, goodwill she wings
To conjure words for all to sing.'

Goldfinch

Magic tradition: Europe and the Americas
Sacred meaning: joy, renewal, richness, charm
and goodwill

There is a medieval legend that when Christ was carrying
the cross to Calvary, a goldfinch plucked a thorn from
the crown on his head (goldfinch adore thistles and other
thorny seeds), and spots of Christ's blood splashed on to
the bird's plumage to give it its red markings. This delightful little bird is often pictured with Christ or the Madonna
in Renaissance art, and given the bird's beautiful, high-
pitched song and happy, flirtatious, darting flight, it's not
surprising the collective noun for goldfinches is a charm.
An Iroquois folk legend tells how a fox repaid the kindness
of some dull brown songbirds by painting their bodies
gold, but before he could finish painting all their feathers
the birds in their joy darted away like rays of sunshine to
become goldfinches. A European Valentine's Day tradition
recounts that if the first bird a young maiden sees on that
day is a goldfinch, she is sure to marry a wealthy man.

RITUAL TO CONNECT TO THE MAGIC
OF THE GOLDFINCH'S SONG

If you have ever listened to the beautiful sound of a charm
of goldfinches as they swoop suddenly down to feed on
a thistle in your garden, then you will know the joy it

brings and how this can enrich your spirit. However, it could be a long wait for goldfinches to come to you for the purposes of this ritual, and not at all practical if you don't have access to a garden or outside space, but you can hear them in another way. You have already experienced the sound of birdsong in part two (page 46), but this is a different way of 'hearing' it.

You will need:

> 1 red candle
> 1 yellow or gold candle
> image of a goldfinch
> recording of Vivaldi's 'Goldfinch' flute concerto

1. Light the candles to remind you of the joy of the gold and red of the little goldfinch, and turn on the music. Whether you listen to only part of this concerto or to all of it, this piece of classical music gives grace to these charming birds, and will enrich your spirit in the process.
2. Now, focus on the image. (If you like, you can paint one yourself, and really connect to the bird in this way too.)
3. Visualise yourself in a garden with a charm of goldfinches. They are bringing you sunshine rays of goodness and a wealth of happiness as they sing, swoop in and out between the trees, the plants and even your fingers.
4. Listen for as long as you like to the concerto (it

lasts about ten minutes), aware that as you move with the music, you move with the happiness of the goldfinch.

GOLDFINCH CHARM OF THANKS

Give back to goldfinch the golden good-heartedness that you want to share with this planet by carrying out this ritual, which is adapted from an old nursery rhyme that still brings joy to every child – and will bring joy to the child in you too! Perform this ritual in spring, summer or autumn.

You will need:

gold nail varnish
compass, e.g. on your phone (optional)

1. Paint gold nail varnish on your two index fingernails.
2. Stand in the open countryside or a tranquil garden. Get your bearings (with a compass if necessary) so that you know where to face north, east, south and west.
3. With your arms outstretched, turn first to the north. Point the painted index fingers of both your hands forwards and say the first two lines of the following charm:

> *'Two little goldfinches sitting on a tree,*
> *One named Joyful, the other named Glee.*
> *Fly away Joyful, fly away Glee,*
> *Come back Joyful, come back Glee.'*

4. For the third line of the charm – 'Fly away Joyful, fly away Glee' – quickly pull your fists back behind your head and point your middle fingers behind your head.
5. For line four – 'Come back Joyful, come back Glee' – make your hands back into fists, then point your index fingers and stretch your arms out in front of you to reveal your gold nails once more.
6. Repeat these actions at each direction of the four compass points to share your delightful goldfinch charm with the world.

Dolphin

Magic tradition: Europe, Hindu and the Americas
Sacred meaning: playfulness, celebration, altruism, harmony and compassion

The dolphin is renowned for being one of the most sociable and communicative of animals, as they leap and play alongside the bows of passing ships. Friendly dolphins were thought by ancient Mediterranean civilisations to be messengers from the gods. In Greek mythology, Taras, son of the ocean god Poseidon, was saved from a sinking ship by a dolphin and the Spartans then built the city of Taras to honour the mythical hero. Dolphins appear throughout Greek art, depicted as helpers, guides and oceanic lifesavers. Another tale tells of how the poet Arion was also safely carried to land by a dolphin after a shipwreck. In Hindu mythology, the river dolphin is associated with the goddess Ganga, who guards the River Ganges. Her mount, Makara, is sometimes depicted as a dolphin. In South American folk tradition, the *boto*, a species of freshwater dolphin that live in the Amazon River, are believed to be shape-shifters, or *encantados*, who in human form seduce young women.

RITUAL TO CONNECT TO THE DOLPHIN'S PLAYFUL SPIRIT

Perform the following ritual to invoke compassion and altruism by connecting with the spirit of the dolphin.

You will need:

  bowl of water
  2 aquamarine crystals
  oil diffuser or tea-light candle
  2 drops bergamot essential oil
  2 drops eucalyptus essential oil
  2 drops ocean or sea pine oil

1. Place your bowl of water in your sacred space or garden and gently put the two crystals in the water so they sink to the bottom.
2. Light your oil diffuser and add the essential oils. If you're using a tea-light candle, drip the oil into the bowl of water instead. As you do so, say this affirmation: 'I will be as compassionate, kind, accepting and as joyful as the dolphin. By invoking the dolphin's spirit of playfulness, I ignite my own positive energy and sense of altruism for all that is on this Earth.'
3. Gaze into the bowl for a few minutes and make slow circles on the surface with your fingers. You will soon see your crystals dance like dolphins, awakening you to their song.

DOLPHIN RITUAL OF THANKS

If you are able to go down to your nearest seashore for this ritual of thanks, all the better. If not, find an image of the ocean, the sea or a seascape that you truly love.

1. As you gaze across the sea, or your image, stand straight, firm and tall. Hold your hands high up above your head, palms facing one another (as in the yoga pose *Urdhva Hastasana*), then bring your hands down in a prayer pose to your chest. You are now greeting the ocean before you and all that live in it.
2. As you stand still, gaze towards the horizon for a

few minutes and imagine dolphins leaping in joy across the seascape; then lower your arms to either side of your body with your palms facing the sea.

3. Repeat the following words: 'This salutation honours all life of the ocean and the dolphins who bring us the joy of it. I return this joy now.'

4. Raise your hands with palms together in prayer pose to your chest again, bow slowly and smile. You are now a joy-bringer for the world's dolphins and will help to revive their spirited power.

Hare

Magic tradition: Europe, Asia and the Americas
Sacred meaning: intuition, moonlight, illumination, fortune and unpredictability

The elusive hare nests among the low grasses and mounds of windswept fields and hills. Hares don't run in straight lines when they are being hunted or chased; they run haphazardly and usually head uphill to outwit their attackers. In some North American traditions, the hare was thought to be a trickster spirit, while this swiftest of European mammals symbolised lust and fertility to the ancient Greeks and Romans. In Chinese, Japanese and Mexican mythology, the Moon was thought to be the home of a spiritual hare who ruled the lunar orb. A curious symbol known as the 'Three Hares' is found carved or depicted at many sacred sites across Asia and Europe. The bizarre motif shows three hares chasing one another in a circle. Each of the ears is shared by two hares, so that only three ears are shown. This correlates to the triskele symbol of Celtic belief, which represents the balance of the three mythological realms of land, sea and sky. To the Chinese, a similar symbol represents peace, love and tranquillity, whereas in pagan and medieval Christian traditions it is associated with three specific lunar phases of New Crescent Moon, Full Moon and Dark of the Moon. Known for its crazy courtship ritual, the elusive and mysterious hare shows us the way to growing enlightenment (New Crescent Moon), self-realisation (Full Moon) and deepest insight (Dark of the Moon).

RITUAL TO CONNECT TO THE HARE'S LUNAR PATHWAY

Use this ritual to connect to the hare's lunar pathway and gain deeper insights. It's best performed on the evening of a New Crescent Moon.

You will need:

3 white candles
3 moonstones
pen or pencil and paper

1. Light the three candles and place them in a triangle before you. Take the three moonstones and place one beside each candle.

2. Now, taking your piece of paper, draw a Waxing Moon at the top of it. This can show any stage of the Waxing Moon, all the way from the New Crescent to Full. It doesn't matter how big or small it is – whatever size you feel best represents the Moon.

3. Then, at the bottom, mark three 'hares' in a row with crosses, letters or you can even sketch three hares. Make sure that they are spaced out evenly along the page. Bear in mind that this doesn't have to be a masterpiece, even a few squiggles will be enough to connect you to the hare's magic. You can even just write 'Hare' three times.

4. Next, focus on the candles, take the three moonstones in one hand and say,

    'These three hare pathways to the Moon,
    On this my way I go quite soon;
    I see the swiftest of them all,
    My charm revealed, my power restored.'

5. Place the moonstones on each of your hares or markers, then take up your pencil and draw spiralling, curving, whirling lines from each hare up to the Moon. Let your intuitive self take over as your hand traces the line into and around itself, creating your own unique pathways to the Moon.

6. Once you have completed your moonlit pathways, fold the paper and keep it under your pillow for

one lunar cycle. You will now be aligned to the hare's powers of deep illuminating insights.

HARE RITUAL OF THANKS

To see a hare in the wild is very rare, but if by chance you do, make a wish and the hare will carry it for you along the path he makes and send your wish out into the universe. If it is unlikely that you will see a hare in the wild, you can always perform the following ritual of thanks.

You will need:

image, sculpture or other representation of a hare
3 white candles

1. Take your hare representation and place it in the south corner of your home or sacred space. This will maximise the illuminating energy of the hare.
2. Light three candles and send out blessings by repeating: 'Swifter than most, gentler than all, with light and love I bless you, hare.'

Wolf

Magic tradition: Europe, Japan and North America
Sacred meaning: instinctive, free-thinking, self-reliant and independent

Sacred to the Greek god Zeus and the Norse god Odin, historically the wolf was considered to be a malefic influence, and, in Christian lore, was associated with the devil. While feared as a predator, it is also admired for its ability to be either a lone wolf or leader of a pack, not forgetting its strength, courage and wisdom. Among European and Northern American peoples, wolves were often associated with witchcraft; and other superstitions sprang up around them, such as werewolf legends, or lycanthropy, whereby a human shape-shifts into a wolf. In Roman mythology, a she-wolf nursed the abandoned twins, Romulus and Remus, one of whom, Romulus, became the founder of Rome. The archetype of the wolf is not only of a predator but also a protector, both of which reside within us all. As a spirit guide, the wolf is considered to be a messenger who, when called on, brings self-reliance, bravery and an ability to discover our own pathway.

RITUAL TO ALIGN TO THE SPIRIT OF THE WOLF

To align yourself to the wolf's spirit of courage, independence and forward-thinking, go to a green space and perform the following ritual when there is a Waxing Moon.

You will need:

> 1 piece of citrine
> 1 moonstone

paper bag
trowel or spoon

1. Gather your ingredients and head out into nature.
2. Find a quiet place, preferably in a wood or among trees, where you can feel a sense of nature around you and where the soil is moist enough to dig.
3. Taking your trowel or spoon, make a small opening in the ground, then place your two crystals in the paper bag and gently ease this into the hiding place you have just uncovered. Cover over with leaves, moss, weeds, etc., as appropriate.
4. As you perform the ritual, repeat: 'The wolf within me be spirited now. With citrine yellow for solar independence and moonstone for lunar instinct, I share in your greatest attributes, so mote it be.'
5. Thank the trees around you for sharing this practice with you, and leave the offering to be charged with wolf energy. Return after one lunar cycle, and keep the crystals safe in your home or garden to promote self-reliance and independence.

WOLF RITUAL OF THANKS

This ritual to return energy and thanks to nature uses oils and plants that are associated with the attributes of the wolf's habitat.

You will need:

- 5 stems, twigs or branches of pine or cedar found on the forest floor (if none available, use any branches or twigs you find on the ground)
- 5 drops of cedarwood oil
- 1-metre (3-foot) length of raffia twine or black ribbon

1. Take the oil and plants either into your garden or preferably out into a wooded or forested part of the countryside. (Any urban witches can do this in their sacred space or kitchen instead.)
2. Find a comfortable place to sit and begin to bind the branches together with the twine while you repeat the following incantation:

'With wood of old and potion new,
I bind intentions to be true –
This oil-blessed stick, this twining done
For all of nature's wolves be one.'

3. Once you have finished binding the bouquet with the ribbon or twine, drip the oil onto it and leave it beside a tree to affirm your connection to wolf magic.

Chapter 9

Landscapes

Landscape magic will bring you in close relationship with the energy of the Earth itself, where invisible electromagnetic forces weave through valleys, silently flash across lakes or still waters, and tumble down mountainsides like torrential streams. We cannot see this Earth energy, but we can see the landscape and feast our eyes on planet Earth. When you listen to the sounds of the landscape, you hear the beating soul of the Earth itself, which also lies within you.

If you wish, carry out the crystal engagement ritual on page 97 again to refresh your connection with nature before working with the practices in this chapter. As before, please be sure to perform the second ritual as well as the first, so that you give back to nature as well as take from it.

The sea

Magic tradition: European, Australasian, Asian and Native American
Sacred meaning: feelings, the future, the past, hidden depths and the unconscious

The sea is our first port of call (excuse the pun!) as we cross the landscapes of the world. In mythology and folk traditions, this magical body of water is usually associated with a feminine archetype or personified as a goddess. The sea covers most of the Earth, yet we find it hard to plumb her depths, vulnerable as we are above and below her waves. Sea and ocean deities are prolific throughout all world cultures. For example, in Inuit mythology, Sedna is the goddess of the sea and marine animals, and is also known as the Mother of the Sea or Mistress of the Sea; while in Greek mythology, the goddess Amphitrite was the consort of Poseidon, the god of the oceans who stirred up storms and tidal waves. Galene, a sea nymph or Nereid, was known as the goddess of calm seas. So it is she with whom you are going to connect in the following ritual.

RITUAL TO CONNECT TO THE CALMING POWERS OF GALENE

To connect to the calming powers of the sea nymph Galene, and to invoke a connection to your sacred self and the sacredness of the sea, it would be wonderful if you could perform this spell by the seashore. However, if you can't get there, you can perform it by placing imagery of a beautiful seascape before you. Red coral was sacred to the Nereids, but for this spell you are going to substitute coral with red agate.

You will need:

1 pebble
1 shell
1 red agate crystal
a handful of sand (or seasalt) in a paper bag

1. Go to your seashore, whether real or imagined, or in the form of the image before you. First, to be blessed by Galene, either dip your toes or place your fingers into the surf or water's edge, and then bow towards the distant horizon across the sea, in honour of her power. (If at home, visualise this in your mind.)

2. Find a place to sit cross-legged where you won't disturb anyone and where you can safely sprinkle sand or salt onto the ground. Place the pebble, shell and crystal before you. Open your bag and

begin to gradually sprinkle the sand or salt onto your offerings.

3. Repeat the following spell as you do so:

'The tide, it turned and turned again,
Three times it seemed today,
As I looked out from pebbled shores
At crystals cross the bay.'

Repeat until all the sand and salt is sprinkled.

4. Now place your hands on each knee, palms up, close your eyes and say: 'Thank you, Galene, goddess of calm seas, for your serene energy which, like the tides of the Moon's cycle, will always help me change.'

5. Take the crystal, shell and pebble, and return home. Keep your red agate in a sunny place to enhance your connection to your intuitive, sacred self.

SEA RITUAL OF THANKS

This ritual unites sea with land, and affirms the balance and oneness of all things.

You will need:

a handful of dried lavender
a handful of dried rosemary

a handful of dried sage
a handful of dried thyme

1. Go to the nearest seashore when there is a Waxing Moon and slowly sprinkle the herbs into the sea, surf, foam or calm water. If you don't live near the sea, place a favourite image of the ocean, waves or surf on a table or on a flat surface and sprinkle the herbs onto this.

2. As you do so repeat: 'I give to you, Mistress of the Sea, the blessing of the land, to nurture and restore the balance between your powers and that of land, as I align myself to your mutual powers.'

3. When you have finished sprinkling the herbs, touch the water or image with your hand, and put your finger to your lips and whisper, '*Shhhh*. Now we are at one.'

Mountain

Magic tradition: worldwide
Sacred meaning: equanimity, balance, oneness, arrival, and yin and yang

Mountain peaks were created by tectonic movements of the Earth's crust millions of years ago, and throughout the world they provide us with a plethora of myths, lore and beliefs. The one thing these traditions have in common is that mountains usually represent continuity, spiritual faith and focus upwards, towards the heavens. In Taoism, yin was thought to represent the dark, northern side of a mountain, and yang the sunny southern side of the mountain, with both sides being united by the mountain itself. Yin and yang symbolise the duality we perceive of light and dark, hot and cold, male and female, Sun and Moon and so on. We see both sides of the mountain, but in fact the mountain is one.

MOUNTAIN SERENITY RITUAL

Try this simple exercise to connect to the mystique of mountain energy to bring yourself serenity and equanimity. For it, you will need access to a place that you can climb up; ideally, a gentle mountain slope or hillside, but if you can't get outdoors, a staircase will work too.

You will need:

1 white quartz crystal (preferably in the shape of a mountain peak)

1. Prepare yourself for outdoors weather if you are doing this in nature. Hold your quartz crystal and begin to walk up the hill (or if you're indoors, the stairs). Take it easy. Your mountain is only as high as you want it to be.
2. As you climb, hold the crystal in one hand, then transfer it to your other hand after ten paces, and continue to swap at each count of ten mindful steps

until you have counted a total of fifty. (If you are indoors and only have a finite number of stairs, return to the bottom and start again until you have counted a total of fifty steps.)

3. Now hold the crystal between both hands and imagine you are on both sides of the mountain and the mountain is one. Hold the crystal up towards the summit and say, 'Thank you, mountain, for bringing balance and self-acceptance.'

MOUNTAIN RITUAL OF THANKS

This ritual can be used to honour these sacred sites and to return the magnificent energy of their presence to nature. Ideally, you should do it while gazing at a real mountain or hillside, but if you can't do that, then an image will work just fine.

You will need:

10 stones
10 drops of spring water
10 drops of sandalwood oil
dropper

1. With five stones in each hand, sit comfortably and gaze upon a mountain range or high hill (either outside in the wild or from a window); or simply focus on a favourite image of a mountain or hill.

2. Focus and meditate for a few minutes on the mountain's power, stillness, immovable force and ancient power. When you are ready, cast the stones gently to the ground.

3. One by one, build the stones up into a mound until you are satisfied with its shape or height.

4. Seal your intention to honour the landscape by dripping ten drops of water onto the mound of stones, followed by ten drops of sandalwood oil. As you do so, repeat over and over again:

   'With all intent your power is set,
   When all realise, your strength aligns.'

5. Leave your little stone pile in place for one lunar cycle to activate the energy. By creating your own anointed peak of stones – however tiny – you will be weaving the mountain's calm composure back into the landscape.

Forest

Magic tradition: Celtic, Norse, Asian and Native American

Sacred meaning: initiation, the unconscious, secrets, mystery, enchantment and questing

Believed to be inhabited by spirits, deities and other mysterious energies, forests have always enchanted our imagination and invoked both wonder and fear. The protagonist of Dante's *Divine Comedy* remarks profoundly, 'In the middle of the journey of our life, I came to myself in a dark wood, where the direct way was lost.' Similarly, the dark forest was a place that Native Americans would use for vision quests to find spiritual meaning or enlightenment. We may get lost in the forest, but it is also a place where we can find ourselves too. Woods and forests were among the first places in nature to be associated with deities. In Hinduism, the goddess of the forest is Aranyani; in Celtic tradition, the forest is the home of the Horned God, Cernunnos; in Greek mythology, wood nymphs were known as the Dryads, while the deities Artemis and Dionysus were both associated with secret groves, wild woods and dense forests.

RITUAL TO ENGAGE WITH THE ENERGY OF THE FOREST

To engage with the deep spiritual energy of the forest, perform the following ritual. It is best done when the Sun is rising, or before midday during the Waxing Moon phase. Ideally, it should be carried out in spring or midsummer, when solar energy is at its most potent. And it's all the better if you can take a walk in a beautiful wood or forest; if not, focusing on an image, a video clip or a work of art would work well too. If you're working with imagery indoors, try to visualise the following steps in your mind.

You will need:

an offering of a stone or crystal of your choice
box or pouch (optional)

1. Walk into your forest, wood or glade – you don't have to venture too far. Just far enough to know you are surrounded by trees. Make sure you know the way back to where you came from!
2. Stand still and listen to the sounds of nature, the rustling of the leaves and the branches moving in the wind. You may hear birds or the buzzing of insects, but whatever it is you sense, know that the magic of the forest is there as an initiation into the spiritual heart of nature.
3. Repeat the following affirmation:

   'I am both lost and found within the magic forest.
   I meet the spirit of nature here, I engage with the
   *   soul of nature here.*
   I find the soul of nature and the soul of myself is
   *   found here.'*

4. Place your stone or crystal in a special spot, perhaps hidden underneath some leaves, weeds or shrubs, or push it gently into the soil. Look up to the canopy of branches and leaves, and thank the forest for its kindness. If working indoors, put the stone in a box or pouch and choose a special hiding place for it in your home.

5. Walk back to where you came from, remaining aware of the spiritual footprint you have made in the magical forest and of the meeting you have experienced with your sacred self.

FOREST RITUAL OF THANKS

Gaze at a distant forest, wood or copse (either real, imagined or using a favourite image), and perform this salutation to the forest to invoke and empower it as a place of initiation and mystery.

1. Stand with your arms raised above your head, your palms facing one another. Stay in this pose for ten seconds or so, then bend your body and swan dive your arms down to the ground. Stay in this position for another ten seconds, then gradually unbend your spine, and stand up straight again.
2. Raise your hands up to prayer pose at your chest. Wait for ten seconds, then raise your arms up to the sky again and repeat this salutation three times: 'The forest is empowered again, and all my blessings and enchantments given back to the soul of nature.'

River

Magic tradition: worldwide
Sacred meaning: life flow, transition, change and movement

Grand rivers such as the Amazon are made up of not only vast expanses of slow-moving water, but stretches of fast-flowing currents, waterfalls and pools. But whether a river meanders through a lush valley or cuts sharply through a deep gorge or ravine, all worldwide traditions have their own local river spirits, nymphs or deities. In Gaulish mythology, Belisama was the goddess of rivers, while in Hindu belief the Ganges was sacred to the goddess Ganga. In European folklore, crossing or failing to cross a river was a sign of achievement or failure, and standing midway on a bridge was believed to help ward off evil. In more esoteric traditions, such as Hermetic magic, the river is symbolic of the great flow and cycles of life. In European witchcraft, the direction in which a river flowed was believed to determine its magical power. Water that appeared to flow towards the Sun was believed to heal, while if it flowed towards the Moon it was thought to cure a broken heart; while river crossings themselves were thought to be interfaces for meeting spirits or supernatural powers.

FULL MOON REFLECTION ENCHANTMENT

If you make a wish when you see a Full Moon being reflected in a river, it is thought your wish will come true. If you have safe access to a river, it's wonderful if you can perform it outside. However, if working indoors, you can use a white candle.

You will need:

pen and paper
a serious wish
1 white candle (optional)

1. Write your wish on the paper and fold it twice
    to seal your intention. On the evening of a Full
    Moon, take your folded piece of paper to the river
    if you can do so safely (please do not venture out
    at night alone). If you are at home, sit in front of
    a mirror and light a white candle to replicate a
    similar atmosphere.

2. As soon as you see the Full Moon's reflection
    in the river, start to tear up your piece of paper
    while you repeat your wish over and over again;
    then scatter the pieces of paper into the river. If
    you are at home, visualise a river. The reflection
    of the candle in your mirror represents the Full
    Moon. Keep repeating the wish, then tear up the
    paper and place it into a wastepaper basket. Blow
    out your candle.

3. Leave your riverbank, either real or imagined,
    and thank the Moon for fulfilling your wish by
    repeating:

    'Lunar light so bright tonight,
    Make my wish come true and right.
    Shine down upon this river's course
    And send desire to seal this source.'

RIVER RITUAL OF THANKS

This ritual will help keep rivers flowing safely in whatever way they must. For it, you will need safe access to a river.

You will need:

jar with a lid
five tumbled or polished stones of your choice

1. Make a positive intention to go to visit a riverbank. While you are there, scoop some river water into your jar, then drop the five stones into the jar too. Shake well as you repeat the following incantation:

   'Oh, rivers flow into the sea, their course is
   *   never-ending;*
   This offering I do give to thee, to bless all there
   *   intending –*
   For fish or newt, for duck or snail, for frog or
   *   bulrush weed,*
   This potion brings you rippling love and
   *   water's clarity.'*

2. Next, pour the water and the stones into the river, repeating the incantation once more as you do so. Now your connection to this most positive, flowing life force of all will be truly blessed and you will have returned positive energy to the river.

Valley

Magic tradition: worldwide
Sacred meaning: protection, abundance, soul-making, fertility and creativity

Valleys are filled with lush vegetation and are magical, fertile places. In Chinese and Taoist mythology, yang is represented by the mountain, yin by the valley; the mountain is dynamic and masculine, the valley receptive and feminine. Similarly, the valley of oneself is a place of creativity and receptivity. It's a place to be fertile with ideas or to feel in touch with the safe haven within yourself. Your safe valley is similar to the one known as Shangri-La in James Hilton's 1933 novel *Lost Horizon*. In the novel, Shangri-La is a mystical, hidden paradise of peace and harmony. The monks who live at the valley's entrance guide any traveller into the sacred refuge of eternal happiness. The poet John Keats wrote in a letter to a friend, *'Call the world if you please "the Vale of Soul-making". Then you will find out the use of the world.'* If the world is likened to a vale, then your safe valley is a mini replica of this place of 'soul-making'. In magic work, we can use the image of a valley to visit the peaceful, soulful place within ourselves, and if we visit a natural valley, we will also feel its protective embrace.

SHANGRI-LA RITUAL FOR RESTORING A SENSE OF SOUL

If you live close to a beautiful green and pleasant valley, then you can maximise the effects of this simple ritual to help you connect to your soul. If you have no access to a valley, you can use an image of one or conjure up a Shangri-La of your own imagining. This ritual is best carried out when there is a Waning Moon, when the lunar energy will enhance contact with your soul self.

You will need:

image of valley (optional)
5 old keys that can be tied together
white ribbon
5 white tea-light candles

1. Go to your chosen valley or sit relaxed in front of the image you have selected. Now take out the keys and bind them together with the ribbon, hold them in one hand and repeat the following enchantment:

    'Five keys free locks to soul's desire
    Within the valley before my eyes,
    As I walk on through Shangri-La
    I meet my true self knowingly.
    Bless you, Valley, for all you hide —
    Enriched with fertile thoughts I rise

To light a candle for my soul
Restore my spirit for the All.'

2. Raise your arms above your head, then sweep them down again as you take a bow to the valley before you.
3. Now light your five candles as a blessing. Stay as long as you like, either to gaze and meditate on the valley's power, or to connect to your own vale of soul-making.
4. Blow out the candles before you leave and take them with you. Once home, place the keys in a safe place as a reminder of unlocking the doorway to your inner valley.

VALLEY RITUAL OF THANKS

To maximise the fertility and abundance of the valley, perform this ritual in two stages. The first part of the ritual can be carried out between sunrise and midday, while the second should be performed between midday and sunset. Preferably do not perform both parts on the same day.

You will need:

a handful of sunflower seeds
image of valley (optional)

1. Go to your valley retreat, whether real or imaginary, and take with you a handful of sunflower seeds to symbolise growth, fertility and the cycles of nature.

2. When you find a suitable place in your valley, walk forward and consciously scatter the seeds before you into the wild. (If you are at home, simply sprinkle them in a spiral shape before your chosen image of a valley.)

3. Repeat the following words: 'I give back to you, the valley, the source of Soul hidden within these seeds. Thanks to this vale to restore all fertility to the Earth.'

4. When all your sunflower seeds are scattered, stop walking, look up to the sky, and finish with this esoteric blessing that unites all things: '*Hen to pan*, the all is one.'

Chapter 10

Sky and Stars

The Earth is as connected to the sky and stars, as it is to you. But most people don't look up at the sky very much except to check the weather, so to engage with the sky and the stars, we need to look upwards more. If you ever have the chance, lie on your back on a grassy bank, beach or lawn, maybe under the stars on a clear night, and watch the stars twinkle and the planets gleam, and the Moon shine down upon us all.

This section contains spells and practices designed to align you to the powers of the stars and sky – and to space itself, where this Earth was created and finds its place in the solar system. The rituals here will help you connect to planet Earth's place in the universe and to understand why it is so beautiful and should be nurtured, for it is the child of the Sun. Remember to perform both rituals for each section – to restore as well as receive.

The Sun

Magic tradition: worldwide
Sacred meaning: empowerment, energy, light, growth, self, strength, ego and will

Without the Sun, the powerhouse of our planetary system, we wouldn't exist. Along with the Moon, the magic and power of the Sun have been a major influence in every tradition throughout civilisation. In high magic, the Sun is symbolic of light, power and awakening; in astrology, it symbolises the potential of oneself and the self we express to the world. In many belief systems, including Babylonian, Egyptian, Greek and Roman, the Sun was a personified, life-giving deity: known as Ra in Egypt, Helios in Greece, and Sol in Rome. In Incan myths, the Sun was worshipped as the divine ancestor of the nation, while in Hindu belief the Sun is the eye of the god Varuna. In Celtic, Japanese, Germanic and some Native American mythologies, the Sun is personified as a feminine deity. In many magic traditions, sunrise and sunset mark important times for spellwork. Sunrise is best for business success, self-empowerment and spiritual growth, while sunset is for letting go, banishing bad feelings, or transforming negative habits. Enjoy the sunlight, it has given you life.

RITUAL TO EMBRACE THE SELF-CONFIDENCE OF THE SUN

Self-awareness and self-acceptance help us to accept and be more aware of others and the whole of the planet in turn. Solar energy magic enables us to be more confident in ourselves, whatever our strengths and weaknesses, and to shine in whatever we do, allowing others to shine in their own ways too. This Sun salutation will enable you to connect to the Sun's empowering energy, so that you can spread sunny joy all around you.

You will need:

> 3 gold ribbons or twine
> 1 piece of tiger's eye

1. On a sunny day, walk outside and find a private space where you can perform your Sun salutation. Then bind the three gold ribbons in a plait or braid, and repeat: 'Solar light, bring me your grace so every day I am aligned to your power, and in touch with my true self.'

2. Now place the tiger's eye on the ground and encircle it with the gold plait.

3. Sit cross-legged before your solar offering and raise your arms above your head and your face to the sky. Make sure to close your eyes and avoid looking directly at the Sun! Bow forward and let your arms touch the ground. Repeat this five times, and then sit in a comfortable position again.

4. Repeat the above incantation and your tiger's eye will be charged with solar energy. You can now carry it with you as a talisman and it will aid you in creating positive results and joyful times. Place the gold plait in a box for safekeeping. You can repeat this ritual anytime you need a boost of solar self-confidence.

SUN RITUAL OF THANKS

Earth depends upon the Sun for its life force, but it also depends on us all to make the world a better place, rather than destroy its beauty. To instil sunshine back into nature and recycle some of that solar joy we have taken for ourselves, do this simple practice.

You will need:

combination of flowers, herbs, grass or any other form of greenery

1. Cast a magic circle around you using the plants that you have collected. To cast your circle, stand and face east. As you do so, thank the rising sun for its guidance. Then begin to turn in a clockwise direction, scattering the plants in a circle around you. Now turn and face west and thank the setting sun for its protection.

2. Standing in the middle of the circle, raise your head to the sky, close your eyes and put your hands together in prayer pose in front of your chest. Repeat the following incantation:

   'With rings of flora round me go
   This charm will ask the Sun to flow.
   With solar light and fertile mind
   For all of Earth this joy to find.'

3. Open your eyes, bring your arms back to your sides, and step out of your circle. Now collect all the plants you have scattered on the ground and place them either on a compost heap, in an organic recycling bin or simply bury them in the soil as a gesture of solar intention and light for all of nature.

The Moon

Magic tradition: worldwide
Sacred meaning: magic, intuition, the feminine, feelings, home and bewitchment

Like the Sun, the Moon is one of the most empowering energies for all forms of magical work. Lunar light is a reflection of the Sun's light, but Luna has her own powers and is responsible for tides, feelings and nurturing. In folk traditions, she is associated with witchcraft and dark magic. As a guardian witch of planet Earth, your connection to lunar cycles will be one of the most potent ways to make your magic happen. Knowing when to cast a spell for success, relinquish feelings, promote family happiness or bring abundance is part of working with the Moon. Work with a Waxing Moon for progress, deliberation, seduction and giving. Spells for completion, fulfilment, manifestation or realisation are most successful at a Full Moon. The Waning Moon is for banishing and letting go, and the Dark of the New Moon (when you can't see the Moon at all) is for acceptance, deliberation, transformation and endings. Lunar deities are usually considered feminine, such as the Greek goddess Selene, but the Moon has also been personified as a male god, such as Sin in Mesopotamian mythology. (As this book is written from a Western astrological perspective, I will be referring to the Moon as a feminine aspect.)

RITUAL FOR DRAWING DOWN THE MOON

By drawing down the Moon's energy, this ritual will help you to align to her magical powers. If you are planning to cast a spell on a Full Moon, it would be wise to practise this energy attractor first.

You will need:

bowl of water or an outdoor water source
a handful of white rose petals

1. On the night of a Full Moon, place your bowl of water outside or on a window ledge and sit cross-legged beside it. If you have easy and safe access to an outdoor water source, you can forgo the bowl of water and sit by that instead.

2. With the index finger of your writing hand, first draw a circle clockwise, very gently, on the surface of the water, then repeat this action in an anti-clockwise direction.

3. Repeat the same process with your other hand, but this time start in an anticlockwise direction before switching to clockwise. As you do so, repeat the following enchantment:

'As Luna's veil wanes cross the sky,
The solar barge at sea she spies;
Slowly now, she spreads her cloak
Across the Sun god's burning wake
Until the Nereids dance the waves
And Helios' light is once more saved;
Thus lunar need occludes desire
So what was lost becomes the prize.'

4. If you are using a bowl of water, leave it in place overnight. The next morning, return to your

water source with the rose petals. Dip your fingers into the water and sprinkle the petals onto the surface – and you will be blessed with lunar magic.

MOON RITUAL OF THANKS

Walking the lunar pathway is a way to give thanks and blessings for all who live by her cycles, including yourself as a guardian witch. The Moon can, of course, be seen in the daytime, but it's at night when she is most vivid and empowering; many of nature's nocturnal beings depend on her light. At each of the following four phases of the Moon – New Waxing Crescent Moon, Full Moon, Waning Crescent, and Dark of the Moon – perform this ritual to establish not only your connection to lunar power, but also your belief in all that is nocturnal and hidden yet alive and inspirited in the dark. Communing with nature at each phase of the Moon will connect you to her magic and that of the universe.

1. Find a path that you can either follow in a full circle back to your starting point, or one you can walk along as far as you want, and then walk back on your tracks to the start. The path should be somewhere you can access safely and it doesn't have to be long – in fact it could be just a garden path if you can't get out into the countryside!
2. At each of the Moon's phases, set off during the daytime along this path. If this is just before dusk

or just after dawn, all the better, but practise caution and never do this ritual alone in darkness. As you walk along your chosen path, repeat the following:

'Lunar power, it grows and wanes
At each Moon phase this my refrain:
Silver Moon above on high
And those who live beneath the sky,
In dark of night their mystery
Is Luna's world of witchery.'

3. Take the path slowly, meditate on your trust in the Moon and all who live by her light. Adjust to the silence or the sounds you hear, and let sounds, smells and things you see be just that — sounds and smells, no more, no less. Like any meditation, be mindful of what is around you, and let it be as it is.

4. When you decide to return, turn around, repeat the charm, and go back to where you started.

The zodiac

Magic tradition: worldwide
Sacred meaning: completion, eternal round, cycles of life and reflection of Earth

The zodiac is an imaginary belt that encircles the Earth according to the ecliptic — the Sun's apparent path around the Earth when viewed from our planet. In Western astrology, the zodiac is made up of twelve 30-degree slices of a 360-degree circle, and each slice is assigned a name, such as Aries or Pisces. However, these slices no longer align to the constellations of the same name due to the precession of the equinoxes (i.e. the gradual changing axis of the Earth's rotation makes it appear as if the stars have shifted position in the sky) and the fact that no one really knows where one constellation starts and another ends. In the Western astrological system, we can determine which zodiac sign you were born under according to which segment of the sky the Sun is in during the course of the year. However, if you were born on the cusp of two signs, i.e. within twenty-four hours of the day that usually marks the Sun's move from one zodiac sign into another, you may need to check an astrological website to find out which sign you are, as the day and time of the Sun's actual transition between signs varies slightly every year. Nowadays, the zodiac is used in magic as a corresponding energy to maximise all forms of spell and enchantment practices. So, for example, if you want to promote career success, you can use the crystal, talisman, symbol, herb or flower associated with your zodiac sign to maximise that intention.

RITUAL TO ALIGN WITH THE ENERGIES OF YOUR SUN SIGN

To align yourself to zodiacal powers, you're simply going to work with your own zodiac sign and a special zodiac magic potion.

You will need:

> 3 drops of sandalwood essential oil
> 3 drops of lavender essential oil
> 3 drops of ylang-ylang essential oil
> a handful of pine needles or sunflower seeds
> phial or lidded jar
> zodiac pendant, ring or earring that corresponds
>   to your zodiac sign

1. Place the oils and botanicals in the potion jar. Leave overnight to steep.
2. In the morning, place your zodiac item into the jar, and shake vigorously. As you do so repeat: 'With this symbolic potion I am aligned to my zodiac sign, and all that is the Sun's path in the sky is my path here on Earth. As above, so below.'
3. Leave in place for twenty-four hours, then take out your zodiac piece. Whenever you wear it you will be empowered with your zodiac sign's powers – or you can simply place it on your desk to empower and remind you that your zodiac sign's qualities are your qualities.

ZODIAC RITUAL OF THANKS

We don't often think of outer space as having much to do with what is experienced on Earth. When we look up at the sky, the planets, Moon and Sun seem to revolve remotely around us on Earth. But it's important to remember that we actually orbit the Sun, and put out positive energy to both its place in the heavens and its apparent pathway in the sky, the source of our zodiac system.

You will need:

wand or stick made of natural wood
compass e.g. on your phone (optional)

1. On a sunny day, go out into the countryside or your garden, where you will be creating a magic circle around yourself. To mark your zodiac magic circle, all you need are a wand or stick made of wood (this will show you're in touch with nature) and some means to help you locate the cardinal points of the compass: west, south, east and north.
2. The astrological zodiac begins with Aries at a point to the east, and moves around in an anticlockwise direction, so to align to this magical geometry you will do the same. First, point the stick to the east and say:

    *'This zodiac circle starts here now
    With ram and bull and twins avowed.'*

3. Then sweep the stick anticlockwise 90 degrees to the north and say:

    *'This zodiac sphere is endless night
    With crab and lion and virgin bright.'*

4. Now sweep the stick 90 degrees to the west and say:

   *'This zodiac round is favoured now
   With scales, a scorpion, quivered bow.'*

5. Then sweep the stick 90 degrees to the south and say:

   *'This zodiac magic begins to fold
   With goat, the bearer, and fish of gold.'*

6. Sweep the stick 90 degrees back to the east – then sweep your stick to the centre beneath your feet and say:

   *'All about me the zodiac plays,
   But now I join the cosmic dance.'*

7. Step out of the circle: you are no longer bound by looking apparently outwards, you are part of the cosmic dance and can look both within and without, and give back your positive outlook on the universe.

Rainbow

Magic tradition: worldwide
Sacred meaning: transition, spiritual connection and new beginnings

Scientifically, rainbows usually appear during wet weather due to the reflection, refraction and dispersion of light in water droplets. This results in a spectrum of light appearing in the sky in the form of a multi-coloured arc. Rainbows caused by sunlight appear in the part of the sky directly opposite the Sun. Folklore and mythology often associate rainbows with bridges and transitions, and the Greek goddess of the rainbow, Iris, was the link between the gods and humankind. Like the wind, Iris could travel the breadth of the world and descend to the depths of the sea or visit the underworld. In many European sacred traditions, the rainbow is a symbol of spiritual development, transition, connection and new beginnings. In Norse mythology, Bifröst was a rainbow bridge connecting the Earth to Asgard (the realm of Nordic gods) and earthly warriors used the rainbow bridge to join the gods during Ragnarök (the Nordic apocalypse) in the final battle.

RITUAL TO CREATE A RAINBOW TALISMAN

Carry a rainbow talisman in your pocket during wet weather to ensure there is always a rainbow shining that can keep you in touch with its sky connection and the ability to cross its 'rainbow bridge' to a better life.

You will need:

    1 length of red ribbon or twine
    1 length of orange ribbon or twine

1 length of yellow ribbon or twine
1 length of green ribbon or twine
1 length of blue ribbon or twine
1 length of indigo ribbon or twine
1 length of violet ribbon or twine
small pouch

1. Plait or twist together your seven lengths of ribbon or twine, which represent the seven colours in the rainbow's spectrum of light.
2. Tie your twist or plait at both ends, and then roll it into a spiral ball.
3. Place the ball into a small pouch and make sure to carry it with you in wet weather to show your solidarity with the power of transition via the rainbow.

RAINBOW RITUAL OF THANKS

Seeing a rainbow by chance is a beautiful, magical experience. To give back to nature you can either:

1. Look out for a rainbow on a sunshine and showers sort of day. If you spot one, speak to the rainbow goddess herself: 'Iris, with joy I find you, with joy take my new connection to the sky above for blessings to the Earth and skies and my own rainbow self.'
2. Draw, paint or design your rainbow, or use any

kind of creative medium to invent your arc – and leave it in your sacred place or garden. Give thanks and blessings to Iris using the incantation above every time you pass by it.

Snow

Magic tradition: Norse, Northern Native American, Japan and Europe
Sacred meaning: transformation, purity, stillness and letting go

The arrival of snow is delightful when it falls silently onto our world, bleak when it whips into a blizzard or breathtaking when it covers the land with dazzling whiteness. Snow creates a blanket, muffling or wrapping life in a static embrace. Ice and snow freeze our hearts, but when all melts and spring returns, the world is transformed. In Japanese folk legend, a female snow spirit was known as a *Yuki-Onna*, a witch with magic powers, unfortunately more demonic than kindly, who stole the souls of those she bewitched. In Norse mythology, there were originally two primordial realms: one of fire, Muspelheim, and the eternally cold Niflheim. Cold realms were often associated with negativity, but for our connection with nature, we are going to use snow's positive energy – that of its transformative power over the landscape through both its ability to cover our tracks and also to reveal hidden joys when it melts.

SNOW ANGEL RITUAL

Be an angel in the snow, real or imagined, and your own inner iciness will melt and your heart will be true for all your future intentions. If you are lucky enough to find snow nearby, or have a trip planned where you can engage with snow, then so much the better. If not, you will have to use your imagination or a little help from a few ice cubes.

1. If you have access to fresh snow, you can make a 'snow angel' simply by lying on your back in it and then moving your arms up and down, and your legs from side to side, to form the shape of angel wings in the snow. If you can't do this literally, then visualise yourself doing it. To help yourself imagine the cold, lie down in a comfortable place and, with your palms turned up, place a few ice cubes on your hands. Brrr!

2. As you move your arms up and down as if flapping your wings, repeat the following charm to align yourself to the power of the transformative energy of snow:

   'When snowflakes fall I gain my strength,
   With whiteness still and my intent
   Transform my heart and melt my pain
   So I can start my world again.'

3. Come out of your ritual, and warm yourself up with anything or anyone you like!

SNOW RITUAL OF THANKS

We can't really help the snow, any more than we can help the wind. But we can put out positive energy and understanding for all who depend on the snow and ice in this world, and any wildlife living in snowy habitats. Think of polar bears, penguins, snow leopards and other Arctic and Antarctic creatures. Their world is disappearing fast, thanks to humanity's folly. We need to redress the balance.

You will need:

1 white candle
1 white quartz crystal
image of your favourite snow scene

1. On a table or your sacred altar, light the white candle. Then place the white quartz crystal next to the candle as an offering, and focus on your snowy scene.
2. As you focus, repeat this affirmation: 'For all who live with ice and snow, this offering will give you all my thanks and connectedness so you can truly be the essence of yourself.'

Chapter 11

Sacred Places

Earth is filled with sacred places. Some are secret places, only known to you (maybe your own sacred garden, or a favourite glade or riverbank); others are world famous for their monuments or special energy, such as the pyramids of Giza or Stonehenge in the English county of Wiltshire. Sacred spaces can consist of landscape formations, such as Ayers Rock in Australia, the River Ganges or great mountains like Mount Sinai in Egypt or the Kunlun range in China, where ancient Taoists found enlightenment.

Connecting to these spiritually powerful places, and discovering that they are pathways to the sacredness of you and of the Earth, can be just as magical as aligning with fauna and flora. By revitalising, empowering and cherishing sacred places, you add another dimension to the Earth's magic and to nature with your own spiritual footprint. Sacred places have a spiritual energy all of their own, and it is there to be shared with you through the practices in this chapter. Take a step and make your footprint – first, in your own sacred garden, a magical space that we discovered in chapter 6.

Your sacred garden

Magic tradition: Asia, Europe
Sacred meaning: a place to be at one with the Earth and the universe

See page 73 for some of the myths associated with sacred gardens. The following practice, for leaving a spiritual footprint in your sacred garden, mirrors the belief in Buddhism that during the Buddha's lifetime, he left his footprint on the highest mountain of Sri Lanka to indicate the importance of the island for his teaching. Now you are going to leave your footprint in your own garden – and to treasure that mark.

RITUAL FOR LEAVING A
SPIRITUAL FOOTPRINT

1. First of all, decide where in your garden you would like to leave your spiritual footprint. It could be at the foot of an oak tree, in a flower bed, an orientation aligned to a compass point of your choice, or anywhere that has significance for you. Even if you are working with a sacred plant pot or unable to visit an outside space, you and only you must decide where this sacred footprint will be left.

2. When you are absolutely sure you know where you want to make your mark, go to that chosen spot. Stand firm for a few moments, close your eyes and raise your hands to the sky in salutation. Then take a step forward.

3. Do not move; stay in position with your arms raised for at least three minutes while you repeat: 'My spiritual footprint is now made, and here will always be the place where I learn to be more of myself and accept the sacredness of myself, my garden (or place) and the Earth as one.'

4. Drop your arms to your sides, step back and bow towards the spot. Now leave.

5. Any time you feel you need a reconnection to your sacred garden or nature itself, stand by your footprint for a while and know you have left your mark on the Earth to understand better your connection to nature.

Sacred Garden Ritual of Thanks

Giving back spirituality to nature may sound odd, as it is already immersed in sacred magic and has its own spirituality. But adding even a tiny contribution of yourself will hopefully bring more balance and harmony to Mother Earth.

1. Stand anywhere in your sacred garden or another sacred outdoor space. Watch the clouds, the flowers, the bees, or the rain – observe whatever is happening around you in that moment. Listen to the sounds, touch the grass, or smell the fragrances – good or bad.

2. This is an act of mindfulness of nature's soul, so now give back some of the sacred garden of your inner self. Repeat: 'What I am and who I am is sacred to me, but I give you some of myself, so that we can all find harmony and create a sanctuary for everything on this planet, here in this sacred garden of the universe.'

Ley lines

Magic tradition: worldwide
Sacred meaning: connection, balance, harmony and faith

Ley lines are invisible, straight lines of energy which connect various historic or pagan structures and landmarks that are thought to have mystical or supernatural powers. In the 1920s, British author, photographer and amateur archaeologist Alfred Watkins discovered them and believed they were ancient trade routes. This idea was later developed by some esoteric traditions, who believed that ley lines align with specific Earth energies and supernatural hotspots. This is similar to a spiritual belief of Aboriginal peoples known as 'The Dreaming', which includes a series of ancestral stories about the supernatural creator-beings and how the continent is criss-crossed by their invisible 'Dreamings' or ancestral tracks. The ancient Chinese art of feng shui also talks about flow or lines of negative and positive energy that must be harnessed or redirected to create a harmonious environment. Well-known ley lines include a network of fourteen or more lines that link up Stonehenge to other pagan sites in southern England. Centrally located, Stonehenge is seen as a kind of energy portal or powerful vortex.

RITUAL TO CREATE YOUR OWN LEY LINES

To draw on this kind of Earth energy, you are going to create your own ley lines. Perform this practice during a Full Moon to amplify your connection to the Earth and lunar energies.

You will need:

map of your area
1 white candle
pen or pencil and paper
3 pieces of aventurine or aquamarine

1. On a map, find three places that you know well –
   perhaps your home, your nearest supermarket or
   your favourite park or beach.
2. Light your candle and draw a rough sketch of these
   three points on your piece of paper. The distance
   between the points or what direction they're
   situated in doesn't matter – ley lines aren't about
   compass points, they are about connections.
3. Now draw straight lines between your points to
   connect them up and place the three crystals on
   each of the three points.
4. Write beside each point: 'This crystal is for connection to the pathway around the planet Earth.'
5. Finally, blow out the candle and keep your ley line
   map as a connection to the pathway of the invisible
   energies of the world.

Ley Line Ritual of Thanks

If you know of local ley line hotspots that you can visit,
so much the better. If not, you can track and trace ley
lines on the internet, visit them in your mind and feel an

intuitive sense of being in touch with the place. You can walk any part of the ley line you like – literally or in your imagination – as long as it is a place you feel drawn to. Here is a simple ritual to confirm your connection with the energy as you walk.

You will need:

real or imaged access to a ley line
lavender flowers

1. Set off down your chosen route and scatter lavender flowers along the way.
2. Rejoice in the pathway as you walk by repeating this affirmation:

'Along this way my work be done,
All negative thoughts by all be gone,
With light of day I see the place
To bring me close to lines of Faith.'

Labyrinth

Magic tradition: Greek, Asian, Norse and Native American
Sacred meaning: discovery, the unconscious, self-realisation, spiritual arrival

In literature, the labyrinth first appears in the Greek mythological story of the Minotaur. On the order of

King Minos of Crete, an elaborate maze was designed by the architect Daedalus and his son Icarus, with the sole purpose of containing a monstrous beast, half man, half bull, known as the Minotaur. In medieval Christianity, labyrinths were often found in cathedrals or churches in the form of a maze drawn on the floor; they are designed to help pilgrims discover their spiritual selves by walking into the centre of the labyrinth. The labyrinth combines the imagery of the circle and the spiral, creating a meandering path with individual purpose. Representing a journey to our own centre, it invites us to return to the tangible world once we have discovered our spiritual self.

RITUAL TO WALK THE LABYRINTH AND FIND YOURSELF

Labyrinths have long been used as tools for meditation and prayer. Here, one will invite you to find your own sacred magic. There are many labyrinths scattered across the world, but it's not exactly easy to get to them, so for this practice you will have to use your imagination.

You will need:

> pen or pencil and paper
> crystal, herb or flower of your choice

1. Close your eyes and imagine a labyrinth or a maze. Without looking at the piece of paper, start to

draw it. Your hand may wander in many directions, but it doesn't matter. Continue for a minute or so, tracing a line with your pen or pencil all over the paper without taking it off the page. You don't have to worry about beginnings and endings, just the process of doing the drawing. When you are ready, stop. Place down your pen or pencil and open your eyes.

2. Look at your labyrinth, and then, with your finger, trace the line from where you started and follow it for a while. If you get lost or confused, it doesn't matter. If you get to the end or tangled in knots, it doesn't matter! All that matters here is to be aware of walking a pathway with your finger.

3. When you have had enough, take your crystal, herb or flower, close your eyes, and place it where you imagine the centre to be. Open your eyes and focus on this spot on your labyrinth. This is your centre too.

4. Leave for one lunar cycle and you will discover a new spiritual magical centre in yourself.

LABYRINTH RITUAL OF THANKS

The ancient labyrinth of Greek myth was concerned with containing a monster, the Minotaur. You are going to do the opposite by welcoming a gentle spirit guide into your life. By engaging with spirit guides, you are showing goodwill to the spirit of nature as well.

1. Close your eyes and imagine you are in the middle of a labyrinth. You are surrounded by a golden light, knowing that no one can harm you, nothing can disturb you, and that you are safe.

2. You see another warm, golden light emanating from a distant pathway. You know this is a friend, you have met them before in another life or another place, and now you wait for them to come to you. Gently call to them as if you are calling to a child.

3. As the golden light moves closer to you, you see it is an animal that has chosen to guide you. In your mind, ask its name and what it can help you with.

4. Once you have discovered what you wanted to know, or just felt the presence of your comforting guide, thank the animal, leave the labyrinth and return to normal consciousness. Whenever you feel the need to contact this animal guide, imagine yourself in the labyrinth and it will come to you.

Crossroads

Magic tradition: European and Asian
Sacred meaning: transition, change and making a decision

A crossroads is a liminal or threshold space, usually between two well-defined places, such as when we cross from one room into another room. Crossroads and thresholds are 'in-between places', and exude magical transformative energy. In Greek mythology, the goddess

Hecate was associated with crossroads, wild animals, nature, entranceways, night, magic, witchcraft, herbs and poisonous plants. She was also associated with being between two places. Hecate was identified with the Thessalian goddess Enodia, meaning 'in the road', who also watched over entrances, protected roads into a city and guarded houses and their inhabitants. The symbol of the crossroads suggests we must make some kind of choice when we arrive there. Which path to follow? Which is the right way to go? When we reach a crossroads in our life, we are usually about to make an important transition or change.

MEETING AT THE CROSSROADS RITUAL

This ritual offering to honour Hecate will enable you to connect to liminal energy and to make the right choice when you arrive at a crossroads.

You will need:

map (optional)
pen or pencil and paper
bunch of flowers of your choice
compass, e.g. on your phone (optional)
gold ribbon, twine or string

1. During the phase of the Waxing Moon, plan to go to a place where paths cross. Ideally, this will

be in the countryside, but if that is impossible, you can perform this ritual by focusing on a map. However, you will need to use a strong visualisation technique to imagine yourself there.

2. Before you set off to your crossroads, write down a question on a piece of paper which involves making a choice. It could be anything from 'Shall I take a chance on a new job?' to 'Do I commit to a new relationship?'

3. Fold the paper and place it in your pocket or bag. Take your bunch of flowers and arrive at your crossroads. Whatever direction the signs or the roads are pointing in, face south to align yourself to the beneficial energy of south for making choices.

4. Open the paper and read your statement aloud. To seal your question, wind the golden thread around the stems of your bouquet, and knot it. Then place the flowers by the wayside, while repeating: 'To Hecate and the wildness of nature, I give thanks for this crossroads in allowing me to make the right choice.'

5. Leave the flowers and return home. You will know the right choice to make by the Full Moon.

CROSSROADS RITUAL OF THANKS

To promote the positive energy of all thresholds, crossroads, pathways in the landscape, and to ensure a magical crossing of the ways, perform the following ritual. Do it during the daytime in the phase of the Full Moon to maximise positive lunar power.

You will need:

4 pieces of moonstone
4 pieces of golden thread, twine or ribbon

1. Go to your chosen crossroads, or, in your imagination, to one you have selected on a map. Stand for a few minutes in stillness, holding the moonstones in one hand and the four ribbons in the other.
2. Next, place the moonstones in the shape of a cross to represent a four-way crossroads. Then arrange the threads in the shape of a cross between the stones. You should end up with an eight-pointed star, comprising of the four directions and the four magical elements. At the centre, where the paths cross, is the fifth element of Spirit, symbolic of new beginnings, richness and abundance.
3. Look up at the sky and repeat:

'Four roads they cross, as do my stones,
Four pathways merge, as does my gold,
With eight points made I bring the Air,
Of Earth, Water, Fire and Spirit's dare.
Come down the Moon, come down the Sun
To cross all ways when all is one.'

4. If you can leave your stones and threads in place overnight, all the better to enhance the energy and revive the spirit of magical transition in nature.

Cave

Magic tradition: Europe, Asia, the Americas and Australia
Sacred meaning: sanctuary, containment, secret self and hidden knowledge

In legends around the world, caves have been described as being the homes of all sorts of supernatural beings – from spirits to dragons. They have also been thought to be entrances to the underworld and sacred sanctuaries. Some are decorated with ancient symbols and paintings. The Grotte de Font-de-Gaume in France is covered with depictions of bison, horses, and mammoths that date to around 17,000 BC. The Longmen Shan complex, also known as Dragon's Gate, is cut into the Xiangshan hillsides above the Yi River, and is an extraordinary series of over two thousand caves and niches, which contain temple grottoes filled with Buddhist carvings, pagodas and inscriptions dating from 493 CE. In Greek and Minoan mythology, caves were sacred to many of the gods. The Dikteon Cave is said to be where Rhea gave birth to Zeus; the Idaian Cave, where Rhea hid Zeus from his father, Cronus.

RITUAL TO FIND THE CAVE OR SANCTUARY DEEP WITHIN YOU

The magical cave symbolises hidden knowledge and acts as a sanctuary for that wisdom. This practice is a simple way to connect to the secrets of the universe. You will feel a sense of reconnection to your true self too, and the light of the universe will shine through you whenever you perform this ritual. However, please take extra care to place the candle in a safe spot, on a stable surface and away from any potentially flammable materials.

You will need:

a white candle
mirror

1. In a darkened room, light the candle and place it beside a mirror, making sure that both of these objects are behind you so that your shadow is projected onto the wall in front of you. For a while, watch your shadow flicker and change as it reflects the dancing flame of the candle, or maybe it stays totally still.
2. Now imagine you are in a cave, where you feel safe and contained. What you see before you is a real shadow, but it is not the real you. Can you see the real you in the shadow?
3. Next, turn to face the mirror and the candle, and focus on your reflection in the mirror. Is the

reflection the real you or merely a reflection? Can you see the real you in the mirror?

4.   Close your eyes. In the sanctuary of your cave, you can see neither shadows nor reflections. Imagine you walk out of the cave into daylight and see another world all around you – one that isn't made up of shadows and reflections but pure light. Open your eyes and for an instant you will see the light of yourself in the candle flame. Blow out the candle.

CAVE RITUAL OF THANKS

We would do well to make the planet a safe place, a cave of sanctuary for all nature. For this ritual, we must humble ourselves a little and simply respect and light a candle for the world and all that is in it at each of the major phases of the Moon. (To be sure of the lunar phases, you may need to check a calendar, an ephemeris or the internet.)

You will need to burn:

1 white candle during a Waxing Moon
1 red candle during a Full Moon
1 green candle during a Waning Moon
1 blue candle during the Dark of the Moon

Each time you light a candle, repeat: 'Bless the planet and all who live here, to make this a sanctuary for all.'

PART FOUR

Magical Practices, Charms and Spells

All the spells and charms in this part of the book are concerned with fulfilling specific intentions — whether for self-improvement, prosperity or success. Maybe you are looking for love, or want to commit to a relationship, or are craving a deeper spiritual connection? Here you will find spells and rituals for everything from improving your relationships and manifesting desired outcomes, to achieving positive well-being and spiritual healing.

If your intentions are for the highest good of all, by embracing magic work you will simultaneously empower nature with your goodwill too, and as you flourish, so will the planet.

Chapter 12

Self-Empowerment and Well-Being

The collection of spells and rituals in this chapter focus on personal growth and well-being, and will allow you to replenish the planet with beneficial energy at the same time as improving your own circumstances. The practices draw upon the five categories that we worked with in Part Three: flora, fauna, the landscape, the heavens and other sacred places. By connecting to nature's magic, you will discover ways to honour your own needs and work with earth's blessings to help you find success, attract opportunities and invite goodness into your life. In doing so you can give back to the Earth too. Self-empowerment is not just about feeling confident, but about having the confidence in the world around you and knowing that it will be there for you when you need to draw on its magic – but always remember that it's a reciprocal relationship, so do make sure to give back graciously.

Flora

Sunflower

Magic tradition: Europe and North America
Sacred meaning: joy, positivity, self-love, progress and empowerment

Sunflowers are the perfect embodiment of their name. They grow best in bright sunlight, and when young, before they are in full bloom, they turn their heads to follow the path of the Sun – from dawn in the east to sunset in the west in the Northern Hemisphere. This 'heliotrophic' nature is the root of their Latin name, *helianthus* (sun/flower). In Greek mythology, the nymph Clytie fell in love with Apollo, the god of light. After he rejected her, she spent every day turning her head towards the Sun in the hope that he would notice her – but he never did. Yet Clytie remained vibrant, positive and constant in her faith for him. That's why the sunflower is the perfect symbol of self-esteem, belief, joy and empowerment.

SUNFLOWER SPELL FOR SELF-ESTEEM

This practice is best carried out in an outdoor space where the Sun will shine full down on you at midday. (Please wear appropriate Sun protection when working in this way.) If that's not possible, you can create a special space in your home by attaching an image of the Sun to a wall or ceiling.

You will need:

> 60-centimetre (2-foot) length of golden
> twine or ribbon
> 12 sunflower seeds

1. If you are working outside, let the Sun shine on you and open yourself to its power. Next, lay the ribbon or twine in a circle and focus on its centre. Imagine it to be the world; then imagine it to be the Sun or a sunflower waiting to burst into bloom.
2. Now place the seeds, one by one, into the middle of the circle to represent the twelve signs of the zodiac through which the Sun passes.
3. Repeat the following charm to bring yourself personal fulfilment and give goodness to the world at

the same time: 'With this sunflower circle, I bring myself the joy and light of all that is in the universe.'

4. Sit for a moment in gratitude, then unwind the circle, take the sunflower seeds and store them away safely. Keep the seeds in the same place for twenty-four hours to promote all aspects of the Sun's power for renewed self-esteem.

Birch tree

Magic tradition: Celtic, Norse, Hindu, Wicca, Native American and Asia
Sacred meaning: courage, new beginnings and opportunity

In the Northern Hemisphere, the beautiful birch tree has been used to make everything from canoes and dyes, teas and syrups, to cradles and oils for treating skin conditions. In European folk medicine, birch tree sap is a remedy for urinary infections, while the leaves can be used as an antiseptic or diuretic potion. Ruled by the planet Venus, the birch tree is used in magic traditions to symbolise fresh starts, courage and the potential to create new spiritual or emotional directions. In Celtic magic, brooms made of birch branches were used to brush out the old year after the winter solstice, while drinking birch beer was thought to banish evil. The seeds of the silver birch are believed to grow anywhere they fall, which is why the tree is associated with manifesting opportunities – as long as you seize the moment.

BIRCH SPELL TO BRING ABOUT NEW OPPORTUNITIES

Embrace the spirit of the birch to bring yourself new opportunities and to give nature a new beginning too. If you don't have access to a real birch tree, you can use your favourite photo of one, or a simple sketch that you have drawn yourself.

You will need:

pen or pencil and paper

1. On a day in the Waxing Moon phase, write '*Carpe Diem*' (Latin for 'seize the day') on your piece of paper. Then fold the paper four times and take it with you to your birch. If you're working indoors, place your folded piece of paper on top of your selected image or sketch. You will then need to close your eyes and picture that you are interacting with the birch for the rest of the ritual.

2. Sit beneath the tree for a few moments to find stillness, and then unwrap your folded note. Trace the same words on the bark of the tree with your fingertip, then say: 'With grace and respect, I will now take the opportunity to be self-empowered by your energy, and will return all my positivity and well-being in the days to come.'

3. Hold the note against the tree and repeat: '*Carpe diem, carpe diem, carpe diem.*'

4. Refold your note and keep it in a safe place. Within one lunar cycle, you will be ready to take up any fresh opportunity that comes your way.

Angelica

Magic tradition: Northern Hemisphere
Sacred meaning: clarity, self-worth, good luck and protection

In British folk tradition, angelica was once known as 'ait-skeiters' or 'oat-shooters' by children, as a handful of oats can be blown through the hollow stems like a pea-shooter. According to legend, the plant was called 'angelica' because of its angelic properties, which protect against all evil, as revealed to a fourteenth-century monk by the Archangel Michael. The stems are best known for being candied with sugar and used in baking, while the aromatic root can be used as a stimulating tonic. In magic, the herb is aligned to solar energy, fire, and the planet Venus. It is commonly used for protection, especially against psychic negativity, and is grown in gardens as a lucky plant for the home.

ANGELICA SPELL FOR PERSONAL RESULTS

This ritual draws upon angelica's properties as an enhancer of good luck. Use it to attract positive results into your life.

You will need:

a handful of angelica leaves
paper bag

1. Just before a Full Moon, place a handful of angelica leaves in a paper bag. Take the bag to an outdoor space, where you know you won't be disturbed, and lay the bag on the ground.
2. With your hands, dig a small hole in the soil or make a clearing among the old leaves or weeds, and put the bag of angelica into the hole. Visualise the good luck you desire and thank the Earth for aligning with your wish.
3. Cover up or hide your bag, and leave the area. (If you don't have easy access to a space outdoors, bury the paper bag of angelica leaves in a small pot of soil and leave in place for one lunar cycle to activate the energy.)
4. By the next Full Moon cycle, you will begin to see positive results in all areas of your life.

Garden sage

Magic tradition: Native American, Europe and Asia
Sacred meaning: brain-power, wisdom-boosting and wish-fulfilment

Sage was known to the Romans as *salvia*, meaning 'saving', and is used in magic to restore clarity of vision, evoke wisdom, protection and to grant wishes. *Salvia officinalis* (common or garden sage) grows throughout the world and can be used for smudging for home protection and removal of negativity (see page 59). Its rarer relative, white sage, is used in Native American and shamanic practices. Instead of purchasing a ready-made smudging stick, try making your own by cultivating sage and harvesting its leaves. In doing so, you will grow closer to the plant's powers. In English folklore, it was believed that if sage grew well in the garden, then the wife would call the shots at home! Taken as a herbal tea, sage is thought to help with anxiety, depression, boost brain cells and enhance memory. In magic traditions, working with sage similarly brings clarity of mind and fresh insight and fulfils desires.

SAGE SPELL TO FULFIL A WISH

Draw upon the powers of sage to find clarity and fulfil your desires.

You will need:

> 3 large sage leaves
> a fine needle

1. On the evening of a Waxing Moon, think long and hard about what you want to wish for. Make sure it is phrased as a positive wish, rather than a negative one; for example, you might say, 'I wish

for success', rather than, 'I wish I wasn't so bored.' Make the wish as short and direct as possible, as you are going to inscribe it with your needle onto one of the sage leaves.

2. Once you have written your wish onto a sage leaf, take the other two leaves and wind them round and round the inscribed leaf, before fastening all three together with the needle.

3. Leave the little bundle on a window ledge until the Full Moon. On the night of the Full Moon, remove the needle and burn the sage leaves to seal your intention to the universe. Your wish will come true by the next Waxing Moon.

Fauna

Dragonfly

Magic tradition: worldwide
Sacred meaning: self-acceptance, metamorphosis, compassion, authenticity, being candid and living in the here and now

With iridescent wings and the ability to fly with seeming minimal effort, the sparkling, darting dragonfly symbolises change and self-realisation in almost every part of the world. Among Native American peoples, dragonflies represent swiftness and activity; for the Navajo, they symbolise pure water. In Japan, the dragonfly is associated with autumn and is a symbol of courage, strength and happiness. However, dragonflies have sometimes been considered omens of bad luck in European mythology. In English folklore, the dragonfly was once known as 'the devil's darning needle', as it was believed to sew up the mouths and eyes of liars and cheats. Today, the beautiful dragonfly is a symbol of living in the moment and the acceptance of one's choices.

DRAGONFLY ENCHANTMENT FOR INNER TRUTH

Align to the magic of the dragonfly if you wish to know who you truly are and what you want.

You will need:

1 blue candle
1 white candle
1 green candle
1 blue crystal (e.g. celestite)
1 white crystal (e.g. quartz)
1 green crystal (e.g. malachite)

1. Place the three candles in a row, with the same colour crystal in front of each. Once they are in place, light the candles.
2. Now gaze at the crystals and you may see the flicker of the candles dancing in the stones, like

a dragonfly darting between reeds. The longer you observe the flame, the more you will see the dragonfly.

3. After a few minutes, repeat the following incantation:

'The dragonfly dances in the flames
With blue, with green, where colours reign;
Blow out the candles, then jewels be given
Empowering choices and free transition.'

4. Blow out the candles, and place the crystals in a safe place. You will begin to feel in touch with the philosophy of living in the moment, blessed by the spirit of the dragonfly.

Owl

Magic tradition: worldwide
Sacred meaning: wisdom, intuition, insight, communication, mystery, stealth, visionary and occult

This mysterious nocturnal bird, flying silently through the night, winging past the glow of a Full Moon, is regarded with both fear and awe. Because of the owl's ability to turn its head to an angle of 270 degrees, its eyes transfixed on its prey, the owl's magical nature has been associated with witchcraft, death and the supernatural, and also good luck and protection. In classical mythology, the owl became associated with the terrifying Strix, a bird of ill-omen that fed on human blood. In Native American lore, the Apache and Navajo peoples believed that a hooting owl was a portent of doom, while to the Hopi the bird was a messenger and sacred protector from the spirit world. In ancient Greece, the little owl, or *athene noctua*, was sacred to the goddess Athene and was believed to bring luck to warriors in battle. In ancient Athens, the little owl's association with Athene was also sacred to the people of the city, and the bird was depicted on silver coins of the time known as *glaux*, meaning 'owls'. These days, the owl is mostly associated with wisdom and intuition, although superstitions concerning its malefic influence remain in some parts of the world. If you choose an owl as a totem spirit animal, it will help you to develop your insight and discover deeper truths about yourself.

LITTLE OWL SPELL FOR INNER WISDOM

Use this talisman spell to gain deeper insight into yourself and your true motives – and, in this way, to return wisdom and goodwill to nature. (For this spell, the coins should preferably be silver, which is associated with both the Moon and the goddess Athene.)

You will need:

pen or pencil
5 pieces of tissue paper
5 silver coins

1. To invoke the wisdom of Athene and her owl, perform the following enchantment during a New Crescent Moon. On the five pieces of tissue paper, write the following: 'With Athene's Little Owl, I know myself.'

2. Then place the first coin in the middle of one of the tissues, wrap it up and twist off the ends to make a little parcel. Do the same with the other four coins, and then place them in a pile on a window ledge until the Full Moon.

3. On the night of the next Full Moon, unwrap the coins, throw away the tissue paper, and keep the coins in a safe place to enhance all aspects of wisdom and self-knowledge.

Viper or adder

Magic tradition: Europe, Northern and Eastern Asia
Sacred meaning: transformation, fertility, creativity, concentration and self-awareness

Like other snakes and serpents worldwide, the viper (the name originating from the Latin *vipera*, meaning 'alive and bringing forth') is a powerful symbol of the instinctive self and transformation. Known as the common adder in Great Britain, it is the only venomous snake in most of northern Europe. According to British folklore, if an adder is discovered in a clump of cow parsley, the snake will uncoil to reveal a magic stone to the seeker. The 'viper's stone', also known as the Glain Neidr or the Maen

Magl, was a sacred Druid amulet, possessing many virtues such as healing powers, invisibility and precognition. Like the ancient Greek *caduceus*, which features two serpents entwined around a staff and symbolises healing and magic, viper or snake talismans enhance healing and foresight, and remove negativity from your life.

VIPER CHARM TO BANISH ILL FEELINGS

For self-empowerment, and to rid and protect yourself from the bad feelings of others or from feeling put down, practise this charm only during a Waning Moon. Although it uses cow parsley, which can grow abundantly along country lanes in summer, please don't go out and pick any, as there are varieties of similar-looking plants which are toxic, and unless you are a true botanist, it's hard to identify many of the different varieties.

You will need:

> 1 piece of obsidian or black onyx
> 1 piece of white quartz crystal
> image of cow parsley (e.g. a botanical
>   print or photo)
> 60-centimetre (2-foot) length of black ribbon
> 60-centimetre (2-foot) length of white ribbon

1. Place the two stones side by side on your image of cow parsley.

2. Wind the black ribbon round them to create a circle. Then wind the white ribbon round the outside of the black one. As you do so, repeat:

'Parsley flowers for snakes is fine –
Bind it round and bind it mine,
Watch them rise and watch them fall,
The viper's sting will take them all.'

3. Leave your charm in place until after the Dark of the Moon, and you will banish all bad feelings whether from within yourself, or from other people's psychic negativity.

Landscape

Coral reef

Magic tradition: Southern Europe, Oceania, the Americas, Asia and Africa
Sacred meaning: self-esteem, richness, diversity and successful ideas

Coral reefs are made up of colonies of polyps held together by calcium carbonate. Their landscape is a fantasy world of giant umbrellas, bushy straggling plants, strange twisting flower-like labyrinths, pin-cushions and exotic mushroom-shaped mountains. Sadly under threat from pollution, rising temperatures, oceanic acidification, overfishing and harmful land-use practices, this extraordinary underwater ecosystem is home to at least a quarter of all marine species. Red coral was prized by the Egyptians, Greeks and Romans, who used it in jewellery and for other decorative objects. According to a Greek legend, when Perseus severed the head of the Gorgon, he laid it on a cushion of seaweed, and the Gorgon's petrified blood turned to red coral. In traditional magic, red coral gemstones were used to promote courage and help overcome fear and nervousness. Red coral also boosts the self-esteem of the wearer and enhances successful enterprises. However, to protect the coral reef, you are going to substitute coral with red agate in the next spell.

SEASIDE SPELL FOR SUCCESS

If by any chance you can visit the seashore and scoop some water into your jar for this spell, so much the better. But if you aren't lucky enough to live by the sea, you can use bottled spring water with a pinch of sea salt instead. Your jar should be large enough to accommodate the agate too.

You will need:

    1 piece of red agate
    1 jar or phial of sea water (or spring water with
        added pinch of sea salt)
    piece of samphire or seaweed

1. Sit beside the seashore, or choose a quiet place where you can visualise the sea. Close your eyes and listen to the sounds of waves, surf or just the gentle swish of the tide. Maybe the sea is silent, but you will still hear other sounds, like gulls or the wind.

2. Open your eyes, take the piece of red agate and place it into your jar. As you do so, repeat:

'In coral reefs is life so rich,
Yet what we do is steal its wealth.
But now I offer this, my truth –
An agate power for me and you
To bring success, to give back more
To stir new life, revive, restore.'

3. Put your finger in the jar and gently stir the water in an anticlockwise direction for five turns.

4. Now, remove the red agate, empty the water and toss (or imagine tossing) the piece of samphire or seaweed into the sea to send your thanks to the faraway coral reefs. Keep the red agate with you for one lunar cycle to promote success in any enterprise and to recycle goodness to the world of the coral reef.

Island

Magic tradition: worldwide
Sacred meaning: solitude, self-understanding, hidden treasure and transition

Although the thought of living an island life may seem idyllic to many, it might overwhelm others with a sense of entrapment or loneliness. When we are disconnected from the mainland by a stretch of water, the strength of our feelings of separation or separateness depends on our individual psyche. Two Greek myths make symbolic allusions to the powers of islands. One is the myth of the vengeful sorceress Circe, who lived alone on her beautiful island of Aeaea, and who lured the voyager Odysseus to her, turning his crew to swine. On another island, Ogygia, the nymph Calypso also fell in love with Odysseus, trapping him with lust and love for seven long years. Perhaps Circe's island, although ostensibly a trap, turned out to be a positive initiation for Odysseus by forcing him to work out how to free himself and his men; while Calypso's seductive wiles turned out to be far more dangerous, blinding Odysseus with sexual desire. After seven long years he had an epiphany and returned to his wife, Penelope. As in myth, so in magic: an island is a place on which to find yourself. To discover the real treasure of the island is to find your true self while you are there.

TREASURE ISLAND ORACLE TO REVEAL YOUR HIDDEN POTENTIAL

Here is an oracle using the magical power of an island to find the hidden treasure buried within you. Like any treasure hunt, you will first need a map before you can go in search of treasure.

You will need:

piece of paper
pen, pencil or paintbrush
inks or paints (optional)

1. Drawing on your creative spirit or just a memory of childhood treasure island maps, sketch or paint your own island. You can include coves, ships at sea, mark spots for villages, draw a forest and pathways criss-crossing the island. It's important to make your island what you want it to be.

2. Add a marker for buried treasure, and then plot a pathway from where you land on the island (label this point A) all the way to the treasure (point B). Think about the journey and how you'll get there: will you need to traverse a mountain, navigate a forest, swim across a lake? Will you encounter wild beasts, mythical creatures, or any other obstacles to get there?

3. Once you have finished creating your treasure island map, close your eyes and focus your mind on what gems or crystals you would most like to find in the treasure chest. You may suddenly see gold, rubies, diamonds, moonstones; whatever it is that you visualise will reveal to you what needs to be awakened inside of yourself. The treasure is a manifestation of your hidden potential.

Key to your hidden treasure

Draw a treasure island map and visualise your treasure. Then use the key below to reveal your hidden potential:

- *Blue stones such as blue lace agate, aquamarine, turquoise and lapis lazuli:* to find a spiritual belief system or way of life, develop your intuitive and psychic powers, use magic, divination or ritual to improve your life.
- *Clear stones such as diamonds and quartz crystal:* to be centre-stage or to prove that you're number one by committing yourself to a talent, desire or long-term goal.
- *Green stones such as emerald, green tourmaline, malachite and jade:* to establish an enterprise, create a business of your own, work with nature, and build a safe, reliable home or family.
- *Milky-coloured stones and metals such as moonstone, opal and silver:* to be creative, an artist, a writer, a musician; to develop your talents, discover truths, express your creativity.
- *Red and purple stones such as rubies, garnets, red agate and amethyst:* to show your passion for someone; to be inspired

and motivated by a new career, adventure or express a creative talent.

- *Yellow stones and metals such as citrine, sunstone, tiger's eye and gold:* to communicate, trade, be socially active, transmit ideas and listen to others, and to write, invent, analyse and be verbally creative.

The beach

Magic tradition: worldwide
Sacred meaning: revitalising, inspiration, self-empowerment and self-reflection

Beaches are as diverse as the coastlines they fringe. A sandy beach is often seen as a beautiful, magical place where it's easy to walk or watch the sea, whereas a pebbly beach is considered more difficult to traverse and perhaps not so easy on the eye. But whatever our personal taste for sand or stones, the beach has always been a space to reflect, feel empowered and connected to sea, sky and land. It's a place where we can gaze across to the horizon, leave our footprints in the sand or write a message to the universe. The Greek goddess of sandy beaches was Psamathe, the wife of Proteus, the seal-herder. Call on her in this spell to help to revitalise and empower you with good intentions for the world around you and to feel good about yourself too.

BEACH CHARM TO FEEL
GOOD ABOUT YOURSELF

If you can go for a walk on a sandy beach, that will help this charm to work its magic. But if that's not possible, then visualise a beach you have visited before and imagine yourself there . . .

1. Stand on your beach and wiggle your toes in the sand, or bend down to run your fingers through it to show you're in contact with its energy.
2. Now call in the elements and Psamathe's help to empower you. Turn to the north and say: 'I call in the element of Earth and Psamathe to empower me with good feelings.'
3. Next, turn to the west and say: 'I call in the element of Water and Psamathe's protection to empower me with good feelings.'
4. Face south and say: 'I call in the element of Fire and Psamathe's strength to empower me with good feelings.'
5. Then turn to the east and say: 'I call in the element of Air and Psamathe's wisdom to empower me with good feelings.'
6. Now stand still, turn to face the sea and repeat the following charm:

   'The empty beach, it lies in wait
   For lonely souls who seek their fate,
   Where silver sailors packed with mead

Have turned their minds to eat seaweed
With shells and cockles, samphire too,
A salted seabird sings the blues
When combing surf with dowsing hands
We find the secret in the sands.'

7. Conclude by saying: 'Thank you, Psamathe, for empowering me with the positive energy of the beach, ocean, stars and sky.' Leave the beach and you will feel vitalised and inspired.

Sky and stars

Wind

Magic tradition: wherever the wind blows . . .
Sacred meaning: change, movement, forward-thinking and moving on

The wind has been personified or worshipped in most ancient civilisations in one form or another. The four wind gods of Greek mythology were collectively known as the Anemoi, and they were associated with the four seasons and the four cardinal directions. The major wind and storm god in Hindu tradition was Rudra; while to the Native American Iroquois peoples, Da-jo-ji was the mighty panther spirit of the west wind and O-yan-do-ne the moose spirit of the east wind. One of the few female wind personifications was the Slavic goddess Dogoda, who presided over gentle love and the west wind. In British folklore, wind charms were made by going to a windswept place and tying three knots into a stout piece of rope to capture three winds of varying strength. The charm was then sold to sailors and fishermen to capture the right kind of wind. Although we can't literally grasp the wind, we can feel it as it touches us. It can be cold, hot, humid, dry, gale-force, breezy or erratic. It can destroy our hairstyle or bring a glow to our cheeks, but essentially we cannot trap the wind, or have any control over it. Wild and free, the wind does what it does.

WINDY DAY SPELL TO MANIFEST SUCCESS

In spellwork, we can call on the wind to help us move forward in life and to accept that there will be both blustery days and calm ones – and that all will be well, as long as we trust in and go with the wind's flow. This simple spell for success is best performed on a windy day during the Waxing Moon phase.

You will need:

> your journal
> 4 stones

1. Write down the following spell in your journal:

'Go whistle in a windless sky
Where you're unheard, where all is nigh.
Go whistle on the western wind,
Your song be heard, your love to sing.
Go whistle on an eastern breeze
For there you'll find mere fallacies.
Go whistle on a northern gale
And feel the force rip forth the sail.
Go whistle on a southern air
And feel the zephyr's silken hair.
Next, visit magic's whistling winds
When manifest success begins.'

2. When there is a Waxing Moon, pick a windy day to go on a walk, making sure to take your four stones and journal with you. As you walk, look out for a secret place or patch of ground where you can hide or bury your stones.

3. When you have hidden or buried all four stones, open your journal and repeat the above magical verse to bring yourself happiness. Leave your stones in place for one lunar cycle and the wind will blow gales of success in your direction.

Thunder

Magic tradition: worldwide
Sacred meaning: powerful, but beneficial influence, awakening and change

Thunder is the sound caused by lightning. The sudden increase in pressure and temperature caused by lightning produces rapid expansion of the air, and this expansion creates a sonic shock wave, often referred to as a thunderclap. If you see lightning in the sky and then count in your head the number of seconds until you hear the thunder, you will know how far away the lightning is, at roughly one second per mile away. If thunder is the voice of lightning, then its booming, crackling, rumbling noises or sudden unexpected claps were to the ancient peoples a message from the gods of discontent, warning or caution. To ancient civilisations, thunder was associated with the likes of powerful deities such as Thor in Norse mythology, Zeus in Greek and Indra in Hinduism. Greek and Roman philosophers later attributed thunder to natural causes. Aristotle believed it was the wind striking clouds, while Lucretius maintained it was from the sound of hail colliding within them.

SPELL TO ATTRACT A THUNDERER INTO YOUR LIFE

We often need the help of others, as we can't always achieve everything by ourselves. To ask for help requires a great deal of self-acceptance, yet it is also important to open ourselves up to the voice of thunder — and to accept that someone or something out there is more powerful than ourselves. This simple ritual will invoke good influences into your life and welcome thunder of a very different kind. If thunder is the voice of lightning, you are now going to be that voice and call on a powerful influence to help you in your quest. (But please do not go outside during stormy weather for this practice!)

You will need:

image of a thunderous sky (or watch a storm from the safety of your home)

1. Focus on the image or the stormy sky outside, and repeat: 'With this Voice of Thunder, I now call on all those who can bring me beneficial help – and that their power is for the good of all.'
2. Safely burn, bury or destroy the image to seal your intention to the universe, or quietly acknowledge the power of the storm, and soon beneficial influences will come your way.

Constellation of Orion

Magic tradition: worldwide
Sacred meaning: prominence, reliability, permanence and strength of character

Visible throughout the world, Orion is a spectacular constellation that sprawls across the sky. It includes two of the brightest stars in the heavens, Betelgeuse and Rigel, and is easily spotted at night due to a line of three small stars known as Orion's Belt. This asterism is sometimes called 'the Pot' or 'the Saucepan' in Australia. In South

Africa, the three stars form the *Drie Konings* (the three kings) or *Drie Susters* (the three sisters). In Spain and Latin America, the stars are referred to as *Las Tres Marías* (the Three Marys). The constellation of Orion is named after a hunter in Greek mythology, who was handsome, fierce and charismatic. In one myth, Orion lusted after the Pleiades, the seven daughters of Atlas and Pleione. As he attempted to chase them, Zeus scooped them up and placed them in the sky for safety. Orion can still be seen pursuing the seven sisters across the heavens. According to legend, the seventh sister was thought to be lost, but in fact she hid herself from the sharp eyes of Orion. On a clear night, six of the stars are usually visible to the naked eye. But if you don't look at the cluster directly, you may just glimpse the hidden seventh sister out of the corner of your eye. In natural magic, we use the hunter's symbol of perseverance and seductive power not only in his eternal chase for the Pleiades, but for his eternal presence in the night sky.

ORION'S CHARM FOR SELF-BELIEF AND POWERFUL PERSUASION

Many of us need to persuade others of the value of our beliefs, desires and needs. We need to make it clear who we are and where we are going, and that our individuality or autonomy is important to us – and to do all this without trampling on anyone else's feelings. This simple ritual will remind you that the sky is never the limit when it comes to practising self-belief.

You will need:

star map or image of the constellation
    of Orion
1 white candle
7 gold stars to represent the Pleiades
glue or clear tape

1. In a quiet moment on the night of a Full Moon,
    place your map or image on a table or your sacred
    altar and light the candle to invoke the element of
    Fire for strength, purpose and confidence.
2. Take each of the seven stars (representing the
    Pleiades) and stick them wherever you feel appro-
    priate on the map of Orion. It can be on his belt
    or on the outline of his sketched figure, wherever
    feels right and natural to you.
3. As you perform the ritual, repeat the following
    incantation to seal your intention, which you can
    write down later in your journal:

'Orion's strength is mine to take
For all his power and heavenly sake,
Yet glittering sisters, one, two and three
Enforce the true belief in me.
Four, five and six with tangled braids,
They dance forever 'cross the glade –
the seventh, lost, or to be found?
Within my soul her strength is bound.'

4. Focus on the map for a few moments in the candle-light to soak up the beneficial energy, then fold it up and blow out the candle.

5. Keep your map in your journal or another safe place. Then focus on it whenever you want a boost of self-confidence or if you need to persuade others.

Sacred places

Woodland glades and forest clearings

Magic tradition: wherever there are forests or woodland
Sacred meaning: discovery, clarity and being oneself

In many traditions, forest clearings, glades, glens or dells are magical places for reflection, deepening self-knowledge or discovery. European folklore tells of wild gods who ruled these places, such as the Greek god Pan, wood nymphs and other nature spirits. The Celtic Horned God, Cernunnos, who also became known as the Green Man, was associated with hunting, fertility and wildness. As Christianity spread across pagan Europe, the Green Man was adopted by the Catholic Church to ensure the support of pagan followers. These carved foliate heads became a common feature decorating medieval churches. In 1939, the ubiquitous 'god's head' was dubbed 'The Green Man' by Lady Raglan in a folklore magazine article.

GREEN MAN BOOSTER FOR BEING THE BEST OF YOURSELF

This is a simple charm for connecting with the spirit of the woods to enhance your own positive attributes.

You will need:

1 green candle
bunch of mint
bunch of parsley
length of green ribbon
piece of malachite or green tourmaline

1. On the night of a Full Moon, light the green candle, gather your mint and parsley and weave the herbs into a garland. If that sounds tricky, create a simple bouquet that can be finished with your green ribbon.
2. Place your garland or bouquet before the candle, hold the malachite in your hands close to the centre of your belly, and repeat the following:

'In ancient lore this god was wild,
His nature spirit fine and fertile;
In forest glades we find him now –
His energy empowers my vows.
With this Green Man I find myself
Enriched in spirit with his help.'

3. Place the malachite in the middle of the garland or on top of the bouquet, blow out the candle, and leave it in place overnight. The next morning, take the stone and keep it under your pillow until the following Full Moon to enhance all the positive aspects of yourself.

Sacred wells

Magic: Celtic, Christian, Buddhist and Native American
Sacred meaning: healing, beneficial energy, purity and charisma

A holy well or sacred spring often has special magical significance to the folklore of the surrounding area and its people. Frequently associated with a tale or legend, the water may be attributed with healing powers due to its presiding spirit, deity or supernatural powers. Wells are also thought to be portals to other worlds. Known as 'clootie' or 'cloutie' wells in Celtic Britain, they are usually found alongside a sacred tree. Strips of cloth or rags (called 'clootie' or 'cloot' in Scots) are tied to the branches of the tree as part of a healing or magical ritual. The Chalice Well at Glastonbury, England, is renowned for its associations with the Holy Grail, Neopagan spirituality and the divine feminine. Other forms of sacred waters include Lake Manasarovar in Tibet, a major pilgrimage site for Hindus and Buddhists, and Crater Lake in Oregon, USA, sacred to Native Americans who use the lake for vision quests.

SPELL AT THE WELL OF CHARISMA

Charisma is an intangible quality, yet we are often aware of it radiating from other people, either in the way they act, speak, perform or the way they just are. We all have innate charisma, but many of us believe we lack it. In turn, the belief that we don't have it creates a kind of negativity which then represses the divine spark in us, preventing it from lighting up. Charisma is rooted in the ancient Greek word for 'divine grace', which is derived from the name of Charis, one of Aphrodite's three attendants. To douse yourself in charisma, or rather to revive this quality, all you need to do is to find, create or visualise your own 'Well of Charisma'. Here's how to do this and get ahead in whatever it is you want to acheive.

You will need:

> large glass bowl
> enough spring or mineral water to fill the bowl
> 1 gold candle
> 3 coins (preferably gold- or bronze-coloured)
> small pouch

1. Just before sunset, place your bowl in a sheltered spot in the west corner of your sacred garden, or on a window ledge facing west. Begin to slowly fill the bowl with the water. As you trickle the water into the bowl, imagine you are filling yourself with spiritual goodness and the grace of the gods.

2. Next, light the gold candle and place it behind the bowl, so that the light is reflected and flickers in the water. Drop the three coins into the water as if you were tossing three coins into a magic well.

3. Gaze into the water and imagine that this is the 'Well of Charisma'. Do you see your face reflected there? Do you see the flame flickering? The gold coins dancing? If everything appears still, gently stir the water with your finger and look again.

4. Now repeat:

'With golden light and well so bright
I find my calling is in sight;
I'm filled with waters blessed divine
And so charisma will be mine.'

5. Gaze into the water for as long as you want, then blow out the candle and leave the coins overnight. The next morning, repeat the incantation and you will be oozing charisma.

6. Place the coins in a special pouch and keep them in your guardian witch's store cupboard. Take out the coins and repeat this spell whenever you feel you need a boost of divine grace and charismatic power.

Chapter 13

Relationships, Home and Family

This chapter is dedicated to spells and magic for improving relationships, family and home life. At some point we may find ourselves looking for new love, making a commitment, or releasing ourselves from past hurts. We may be moving into a new home, attempting to patch up our difficult family life, or just keen to incorporate more harmonious energy into our safe sanctuary. It's important, however, not to rely solely on a spell to transform your life. Magic works best when it's supported by your own good intentions and actions. When it comes to spells involving relationships, remember that magic should not be practised for the good of the individual, but for the good of all. Our relationship with a loved one is a reflection of our relationship with the universe, so if you're hoping to improve a relationship, then remember you're also improving your bond with the Earth. If you're looking for new romance, remember you are romancing the universe too. If you are trying to restore family harmony, then remember you are invoking harmony on this planet too. By working with these magical connections with nature, you will ensure there is more love around you personally and more love to spread across the entire planet.

Flora

Wormwood (*Artemisia absinthium*)

Magic tradition: Europe, Asia and northern Africa
Sacred meaning: uplifting, revelation, revival and romantic enticement

Commonly known as wormwood, madderwort and mugwort, *Artemisia absinthium* is one of the main ingredients (along with green anise and fennel) in absinthe. This alcoholic drink was popularised by nineteenth-century Parisian bohemian café culture, and favoured by artists and writers such as Pablo Picasso, Vincent van Gogh, Oscar Wilde and Marcel Proust. The medicinal use of wormwood dates back to the ancient Egyptians, and it was later used in the Middle Ages as a tonic, anti-spasmodic and antiseptic. It has also been used to cure fevers, gout, scurvy, dropsy and for rectifying spirits. In European folklore, on Saint Luke's feast day (18 October), a young girl was advised to prepare a pomade made of wormwood, various other herbs, honey and oils, and apply this to her body, breasts and lips. If she then said a spell to Saint Luke, her future husband would be revealed in her dreams.

WORMWOOD SPELL TO ATTRACT NEW ROMANCE

If you make the magic concoction described here, you will soon attract new love to you – even if you don't see the person in your dreams!

You will need:

> 1 marigold flower
> 1 sprig of marjoram
> 1 sprig of thyme
> 2 sprigs of wormwood
> twine

1. During the Waxing Moon phase, place your assembled botanicals in a warm place to dry out until the following Full Moon.
2. On the night of the Full Moon, take the bundle, bind it with the twine to seal your intention, and hold it close to your body.
3. Now repeat the following:

> 'With absinthe green and herbs entwined
> New love will come and will be mine.'

4. Place the offering in the moonlight, or if it's a cloudy night, a place where there would usually be moonlight, and in the next few days new love may well come your way.

Rose

Magic tradition: Hindu, Wicca, Celtic, Freemasonry and Rosicrucianism
Sacred meaning: love, purity, romance, passion, gratitude and grace

Although most rose species are actually native to Asia, there are many indigenous varieties in Europe, North America and Africa that are widely grown for their fragrance and beauty. The rose has symbolic importance in many cultures and belief systems worldwide. In ancient Greek mythology, the goddess Aphrodite was associated with the rose, and rose oils and petals were used by priestesses and magicians to heal those who deserved her favour. In ancient Persia, rose water was freely added to baths and petals were strewn across the floors, while wealthy Greeks and Romans stuffed their pillows, cushions and mattresses with rose petals to ward off pestilence and disease. In Christianity, the rose became identified with the Virgin Mary and later with the Rose Cross, the defining symbol of the seventeenth-century Rosicrucian movement. The rose has also been a prominent symbol of Freemasonry and the Hermetic Order of the Golden Dawn. Rose petals, rose water, rose essential oils, cut flowers and whole dried buds are used widely in all forms of magical work, especially for love and relationship success.

ENCHANTMENT FOR RELATIONSHIP DEVELOPMENT

Are you looking for love, or wishing to improve a relationship? This lovely spell can help if you have access to a watercourse of some sort.

You will need:

a handful or two of rose petals (either fresh or dried)
pouch or bag
a few drops of rose essential oil

1. On a day in a Waxing Moon phase, place your rose petals in a pouch or bag and then drizzle the drops of rose oil over them.

2. Take the pouch to any place nearby where there is moving water.

3. Hold the rose offering between your hands and visualise how you would like your romance to develop. Do you want exclusivity? More romance and no strings – or a committed relationship?

4. Once you have repeated your wish in your mind, affirm it out loud, before emptying your rose petals onto the water so that they scatter across the surface. Your intention has now been sent to the universe and you will see your romance blossom as you desire.

Hawthorn

Magic tradition: European, particularly Wicca, Druid, Celtic and Slavic
Sacred meaning: happiness, bonding, fertility and protection

This dense, thorny and twisted tree is renowned for its protective powers in European folk traditions. Also called quickthorn and whitethorn in Great Britain, this plant is best known as the May tree because its beautiful white flowers usually blossom during that month. There are many European superstitions about May flowers, with people believing that they bring bad luck if they're brought into the home. However, in ancient Greek tradition, they were believed to promote fertility so couples would be crowned with hawthorn blossom wreaths at their wedding celebrations. A lone hawthorn tree in a field was once thought to be a portal to the supernatural world, or the home to evil spirits, but today hawthorn is grown in the countryside as a protective and ecologically friendly hedging. To dream of hawthorn blossom was thought to predict a happy marriage, while around Beltane fertility festivities, hawthorn blossom branches were used to decorate the Maypole. Today, medicinal hawthorn is renowned for its beneficial influence on the heart and circulation and, although its thorns are sharp, its magical powers can open our hearts to improve our well-being, or restore our sense of love for others and, in return, their love for us.

THORN CHARM TO BIND SOMEONE TO YOU

Use this charm to help make a romantic partner feel bonded to you, and vice versa, if this is going to be to the highest good of you both.

You will need:

1 white candle
7 hawthorn thorns (or 7 pins to represent them)
7 small pieces of paper

1. Place the candle on your sacred altar or a table and light it. Then position the seven thorns in a horizontal line in front of you.

2. Hold one thorn at a time close to your lips and whisper to each thorn: 'By this thorn I seal my troth, and [name of your loved one] in return does too.'

3. Wrap each thorn in a piece of paper and, when you have spoken to all seven thorns, bury them together in a pot. If you happen to live near a hawthorn tree, you can bury the thorns at the base of the tree.

4. Within one lunar cycle, your love for each other will be bonded if this is in harmony with your highest good.

Hawthorn tree talisman to attract more friends

To bring new friends into your life, tie a selection of ribbons or different-coloured threads or twine to the branches of a hawthorn tree and leave in place until these people appear in your life. The different colours represent the types of friend you are looking for. You can use all of them or just one, depending on your favoured character type or purpose.

Blue: understanding, spiritual and accepting
Green: down to earth, reliable and savvy

Pink: gentle, altruistic and youthful
Red: inspiring, passionate and go-getting
Yellow: witty, wise and analytical
White: reflective, imaginative and artistic

Fauna

Seahorse

Magic tradition: European, Asian, Australasia and the Americas
Sacred meaning: courtship, empowering relationships, persistence and generosity

The gentle seahorse is found in tropical and temperate saltwater shallows, such as seagrass beds, estuaries, coral reefs and mangroves. The seahorse's scientific name, *Hippocampus*, derives from the ancient Greek *hippos*, meaning 'horse', and *kampos*, meaning 'sea monster'. It was thought to resemble the head and neck of a horse, while possessing the scale-like armoury of a monstrous fish. In Greek mythology, one myth tells of how Poseidon galloped through the oceans on a golden chariot pulled by a *hippocampus*. Ancient fishermen believed real seahorses were the offspring of Poseidon's steed. Before breeding, seahorses may court for several days in what is known as a predawn dance. These sacred, elusive and extremely slow dancers have tiny fins that propel them back and forwards to one another in a rhythmic movement. Once the eggs are incubating in the male's pouch, the female will go to greet her consort each day at dawn. The intricate courting ritual of the seahorse then culminates at dawn, which is when we are going to work our magic.

SEAHORSE SPELL FOR LONG-TERM COMMITMENT

This spell will help you to empower someone to commit to long-term love if that is the right path for them. It should be performed at dawn during a Waning Moon phase.

You will need:

jar filled with a collection of shells, dried
   samphire and other beachcombed items
image of two seahorses
7 large shells (conch or scallop are best)
7 drops of sea pine essential oil (if unavailable, use
   lemon and cedarwood)

1. Place the jar on the image of the seahorses and then surround the offering with the seven shells, spaced equidistantly in a circle.
2. Pipette a drop of oil onto each shell and repeat the following:

'The lovely seahorse dances in the dawn
And now for me, both bring us love reborn —
A bond is made, empowered and true
For those two blessed, forever us two.'

3. Leave your shells and jar in place until the Full
    Moon and, all other things being well, your rela-
    tionship will be empowered with committed love.

Bee

Magic tradition: Egyptian, Hindu, Minoan, Greek
and Celtic
Sacred meaning: devotion, love, fertility, cooperation
and sweet indulgence

The social nature of most bees, particularly the honey
bee, and their invaluable role in pollination, and thus the
ecosystem, has meant that bees are perhaps more sacred
and precious to us now than they have ever been. With
its innate ability to sense the presence of desirable flowers
through ultraviolet patterning, fragrance or electromagnetic fields, the bee determines whether to continue
visiting similar flowers or not. In Egyptian mythology,
bees grew from the tears of the Sun god Ra when they fell
from his solar chariot onto the desert below. They were
also thought to be messengers from the upper world to
the spirit world. In Hindu mythology, the bowstring on
the god of love Kamadeva's bow was made of sugar cane
and covered in bees. The bee was a motif of the Minoan

mother goddess, Potnia, who was also referred to as 'Pure Mother Bee'. In Celtic myth, bees symbolise the spiritual wisdom of the other world, while in medieval Christianity the bee represented purity and industry. If you have a garden (sacred or otherwise) or you have the space for a window box, why not plant some lavender, chives and rosemary to help bees continue their work and to promote harmony everywhere?

BEE PRACTICE FOR HARMONY IN THE FAMILY

To invoke the same sense of harmonious social inter-action in your home as you would find in a hive, perform the following ritual just before dusk, when the bees are returning to their hives. This ritual will also return posi-tive energy to the pollinating world, which is much needed due to the endangered habitats worldwide.

You will need:

> 5 stones to represent the five elements
> 5 pieces of amber
> 5 stems of lavender, chives, buddleia or
>   rosemary flowers

1. Just before sunset, place your five stones in a circle and then a piece of amber at each stone. On top of the stone and amber, place a stem of your chosen plant.

2. Leave overnight and move the flower stems one place forward, in an anticlockwise direction, each day just before sunset for five days. Leave the magic circle in place and your home life will be brimming with harmonious energy.

Otter

Magic tradition: Celtic, Native American, Buddhist, Europe and Asia
Sacred meaning: playful, joy, enjoyment, celebration, altruism and togetherness

River otters live beside the water in dens known as 'holts' and only enter the water to fish or travel. In comparison, sea otters can spend more time in the water owing to the impermeable quality of their coats. Otters appear in folklore around the world. In Norse mythology, the mischievous god Loki killed the shape-shifting dwarf Ótr while the latter was in the form of an otter. The dwarves were furious and demanded compensation from the gods, who gave them Ótr's otter skin filled with gold. In Celtic folklore, the otter is a friendly and helpful creature, also known as a 'water dog'; and in ancient Persia, where it was revered and protected, the otter was admired for the same qualities. Native American traditions mostly view the otter as a trickster or a companion, while in Japanese folklore otters are identified with shape-shifting evil female spirits who seduce and devour men. Scottish tradition tells tales of

Otter Kings accompanied by seven black otters. When captured, these beasts would grant any wish in exchange for their freedom.

LUCKY OTTER CHARM FOR A NEW HOME

This charm will bring the otter's playful spirit into a new home and banish any lingering negative energy.

You will need:

> image of an otter
> smudging stick (made of sage and cedarwood)
> 5 to 10 clam or scallop shells
> corresponding number of small polished
>   moonstones

1. On the evening you move into your new home, pin your image of an otter on the inside of the main entrance door and leave for one lunar cycle. To celebrate, have a glass of bubbly or green tea, whatever takes your fancy!
2. Light your smudging stick. Now walk around your home with the stick to cleanse all the rooms of negative energy (see page 59). As you do so, repeat: 'Like an otter's holt, my home will be a place of enjoyment and celebration.'
3. Once you have cleared your spaces, place the shells in a clockwise spiral where they won't be

disturbed for one lunar cycle, and put a moonstone in each shell. Your home will be blessed with celebratory energy and good luck for the future.

Landscape

Lake

Magic tradition: worldwide
Sacred meaning: contemplation, mystery, occult and letting go of emotions

Worldwide, there are large bodies of water that are not connected to the sea or ocean. These range from the gigantic Lake Superior in North America to the deepest and largest freshwater lake in the world, Lake Baikal, in Siberia. The latter is also the oldest lake in the world and estimated to have been formed twenty to twenty-five million years ago. Lakes, whether large or small, are at the core of many magical beliefs. In world mythology, the idea of the bottomless lake has been a trigger for legends of monsters, lost cities, treasures, mermaids and portals to other worlds. In psychological terms, the lake is a motif for a place where we go for self-contemplation and revelation. Lakes are also associated with magical feminine power, whether receptive, nurturing and passive as in ancient Chinese belief, or the dual femininity of Arthurian legend. In the tales of Arthur, the Lady of the Lake is both the sorceress Nimue, who leads to Merlin's undoing, and the enchantress who bestows Arthur with the sword Excalibur. Lakes, then, are places of solace and self-reflection, and they can also promise the secret of enlightenment.

SPELL TO LET GO AND LEAVE THE PAST BEHIND

There are times when we cling feverishly to the past, and others when we are ready to let go and start again. If you have been through difficulties and want help in letting go of your emotional baggage or in leaving the past behind, let this spell work some magic for you by engaging with the power of the lake. When casting this spell, it's preferable to sit by a lake, but if that's not possible a pond or even a puddle will do.

You will need:

pouch of 12 stones or pebbles

1. Face the water and focus on the light reflecting from it – the ripples, the scene and the sky.
2. Take one stone at a time from the pouch and toss it into the water, as you repeat the following magical verse:

'They say in love we're often spent
Of words of feelings all that's meant,

But no one told me loud and true
If it's for me or it's for you.
Yet if there was another way
I'd find it out from you today,
For all who saw the bluest stone
They saw their hearts were all alone.
With every love, another's lost,
Take care you now, it's at your cost.
This lake, it holds your memory dear,
With each stone cast I leave you here.
Farewell the past to start again
And in the lake I find champagne!

3. When all your stones are cast into the water, you may feel emotions well up inside you and a sense of loss and grieving for the past. Let them be, let them go, and leave them there in the lake. Whenever you return to the lake you will look back not with anger or remorse, but with acceptance and love for what was. The lake may thank you for that too.

Moorland, plains, prairies and grasslands

Magic tradition: European, Celtic and
Native American
Sacred meaning: loneliness, escape, retreat and
banishment

A moor is a tract of open, uncultivated and mostly infertile land, windswept and barren. The only growth is often heather, gorse or wild grass. Worldwide, this kind of moorland aligns to the Great Plains, prairies, grasslands, tundras and other wild open spaces where little seems to thrive. This kind of land can be bleak but beautiful, lonely but revitalising. For example, far from civilisation, deep in the North Yorkshire moors, sits an eighteenth-century, Gothic-style hunting lodge called Rocking Hall. Now used as a deserted shelter for hikers seeking refuge, this isolated, spooky lodge has as its only neighbour (apart from a smaller derelict building) a strange standing stone, with another perched on top, known as the Rocking Stone. Legend has it that if you manage to rock the top stone, you will summon either demons or a spirit guide – depending on your conscience.

CHARM TO PUT OFF AN UNWELCOME ADMIRER

Using the windblown, wild energy of this kind of desolate landscape and the power of the crystal peridot for creating emotional distance, you can banish, put off, or prevent anyone from trying to get to know you better. To heighten the power of this ritual, you will need to visit moorlands, grasslands or somewhere with a similar landscape. If this isn't possible, you can use a photo as a substitute.

You will need:

　5 pieces of peridot

1. If you are lucky enough to take a walk across a windy moor, find a quiet place where you can lay out your peridot pieces in the form of a pentagram. (If you are working indoors, put your image on your sacred altar or table and place the peridot in the same formation.)

2. After one week, return to the site and turn each stone 360 degrees clockwise. As you do so, repeat the following charm:

'This lonesome moor dulls their desire –
The wild wind blows it far and wide,
Be gone from sight and n'ere return,
My wish fulfilled when stones be turned.'

3. Return the following week to turn each stone 360 degrees anticlockwise, while repeating the same enchantment. As you end the ritual, you will deter your unwelcome admirer for good.

Sky and stars

Venus

Magic tradition: worldwide
Sacred meaning: love, compassion, beauty, vanity and harmony

Similar to the Earth in size and structure, Venus is the

second planet from the Sun and is named after the Roman goddess of love and beauty. Because Venus lies close to the Earth's orbit, she never appears to venture far from the Sun, either setting in the west just after dusk or rising in the east a little before dawn. This phenomenon led to her being known in ancient civilisations as both the morning and evening star, and she was believed to be two separate bodies. In astrology, Venus is a symbol primarily of love in all its forms and rules the Sun signs Taurus and Libra. Yet like her ancient Greek precursor, the goddess Aphrodite, Venus can also be vain, selfish and passionate. For the purposes of most magical work, we use the power of Venus to attract others to us, to create spells for better loving and to improve our own sense of self-love.

SEXUAL ATTRACTION CHARM

This spell will help you to affirm your powers of attraction and seduce anyone in the sexiest possible way.

You will need:

> mirror
> 2 pink candles
> frankincense incense
> 5 pink roses or rosebuds (they can be made
>   from paper)
> 5 sea shells
> pen or pencil and paper

1. On the night of a Full Moon, prop the mirror against a wall on your sacred altar or table, and place a candle on either side of it. Light the incense and the candles, and then place the five pink roses in a circle in front of the mirror and beside them the shells.

2. Take up the pen and paper and write down the name of the one you want to seduce. If you don't know who that is yet, or don't know their name, just write 'desired one'. Fold up the paper and place it in the middle of the circle of roses.

3. Gaze into the mirror and adore your reflection. Yes, love your nose, your eyes, your chin, your lips – and even if you think there is something at fault with your face, ignore it. Love the face you see, because it is that face, that body, that sexual aura that will appeal to the person you long to seduce.

4. Now repeat the following affirmation: 'Venus, I love myself and so someone will love me too; my sexuality is charismatic and empowering, so soon they will be in my arms. Thank you for your kindness.' Before the next Full Moon, your sexual desire will be fulfilled.

Aurora

Magic tradition: Norse, Aboriginal, Inuit, Native American, European and Chinese
Sacred meaning: new beginning, inspiration and success in love

Named after Aurora, the Roman goddess of dawn, this magical light phenomenon is caused by disturbances in the upper atmosphere fuelled by solar winds. More commonly found nearer to the North or South Pole, other types of aurora can be seen in different latitudes. Auroras create a kaleidoscope shower of colours in the sky, and beliefs about what they represent have varied around the world ever since ancient times. During the Middle Ages, Christians believed the northern lights (aurora borealis) to be a sign from God, while indigenous American peoples regarded it as being anything from the dance of ravens to spirit guides who held torches aloft to lead the departed to the next world. Aboriginal Australians associated the predominantly red auroras they saw with fire spirits. The rare aurora sightings in ancient China led to tales of celestial battles between good and evil dragons, breathing fire across the skies. The Vikings believed the northern lights were the road to Valhalla along which chosen warriors could travel to join the gods. In later European magical belief systems, the aurora was considered a symbol of new beginnings and a sign of success in love.

Aurora Charm for Spiritual and Physical Togetherness

This is a colourful charm for strengthening an existing relationship and will allow you to release your inner artist at the same time. However, if you aren't keen on painting, you can use an image of an aurora instead.

You will need:

> selection of colourful paints
> paintbrush and paper
> 1 green candle
> 1 red candle
> 1 blue candle
> 1 purple candle
> 1 yellow candle

1. This is a chance to be creative and paint your own aurora if you wish. You can use any colours or any brush strokes, as long as you are making your aurora come alive on the page. If you would prefer to work with an image that appeals to you, that's fine too.
2. Place the five candles in a circle and light them. Then place your aurora image in front of the group. Gaze into the candle flames and see your own aurora come alive, as if you are literally watching a spectacle of the northern (or southern) lights themselves!

3. Now repeat the following:

    'With solar power and aurora's lights
    Nature makes us bless'd tonight,
    And every day we light a flame
    So in one bed our love is made.'

4. Blow out each of the candles, one by one, to seal your intention to the universe that you and your partner are spiritually and physically one. If you ever feel you've lost that connection, then light the candles and repeat the charm.

Sacred places

Your home

When it comes to relationships, one of the most sacred places on Earth is your home. This is where you can relax with loved ones and remove yourself from the pressures of daily life. Your home should be your sanctuary. For complete harmony in the home and to revive that sense of safety, comfort and security in nature's sanctuary too, perform this spell whenever you feel like your home is in need of a supportive boost.

Visualisation Spell for Harmony in the Home

To give thanks and blessings to your home, to weave the magic of nature into the web of your own life, and to send all that back out into the world with genuine warmth, you need only to sit by a glowing wood burner or fireplace. If you don't have one at home, then sit in your favourite spot in the house with an image of a log fire.

1. Settle down by your fire, close your eyes and listen to it burn. If you are using an image, gaze at it, then shut your eyes and imagine the logs crackling and burning. Visualise the flames leaping and the heat permeating your home, warming it and giving you a feeling of contentment.

2. Now imagine you are asleep and that the warmth of the world and the universe are enveloping and protecting you. Mother Earth herself is holding you in her arms as she warms you on a cold night.

3. Open your eyes and look into the fire, or at your image, and search for the gods dancing in the flames. These are the gods or energies that are going to bring you all the joyful energy you need in your home. They may eventually burn down, settle and turn to ashes, but during this moment your home will be fired with delightful energy and harmonious togetherness.

Your garden

The next best sacred place in the world is the garden you've created. In chapter 6, we looked at how to make this a special place for celebrating all that is holy in life, making it the perfect space for spellwork.

FIVE ELEMENTS PLEASURE CHARM

Here, you are going to lay down the Five Elements Pleasure Charm ·in your garden, which is especially designed to heighten pleasure in romantic relationships.

You will need:

> a handful of small white quartz crystals (for Air)
> pouch filled with herbs and rose petals (for Earth)
> bottle of spring water (for Water)
> 1 red agate crystal (for Fire)
> yourself (for Spirit)

1. In a place in your garden that won't be disturbed, scatter the white quartz. It's important to leave them in place wherever they fall, as they will permeate that special spot with their energy. Sprinkle the herbs and rose petals, then a smattering of spring water over the crystals. Finally, place the red agate in what looks to be the centre of your quartz grid.
2. Now repeat:

'For love of all and all to love
This place is set for heaven above;
Our pleasure rises —
Love is grown
And mutual bonds will be reborn.'

3. Leave the grid for one lunar cycle to enrich your garden with elemental power, and simultaneously your relationship will be filled with pleasure. You can then remove the red agate and keep it safely in your witch's store cupboard.

Chapter 14

Abundance and Prosperity

The spells and enchantments in this chapter are to enhance or promote prosperity and abundance, whether spiritual, emotional or material. But they will also allow you to give back abundant energy to nature. When we hope or expect too much, then we may be disappointed; if we are idealists, then we feel disillusioned when nothing lives up to our ideals. However, if we truly believe in our ability to manifest realistic ideas, plans and projects, then the universe will usually oblige. Just remember to give back some of the prosperity you gain, while making the act of giving as sacred as the Earth itself.

Flora

Oud

Magic tradition: China, Southeast Asia and India
Sacred meaning: sensuality, wealth, pleasure, luxury and acquisition

Found in the forests of Southeast Asia, India and Bangladesh, oud or agarwood comes from the fungus-infected resinous wood of the agar tree and is extracted by distillation from the wood, or by melting the resin to make an essential oil. Throughout the Far East, China and Japan, agarwood is burned and used as a stabilising incense, and in feng shui, it is thought to encourage wealth into the home. In the Buddhist tradition, the most precious strings of beads are made of agarwood, and in ancient Persia the resin was used as perfume. When traders brought agarwood oil to Europe, King Louis XIV of France loved the fragrance so much that he would sprinkle drops of it onto his pillow to ignite passion in his lovers. These days, with its woody, smoky and sensual fragrance, oud provides warm but slightly pungent base notes in many luxurious perfumes. It is associated with opulence, luxury, and with removing negative energies in the home and attracting wealth.

SPELL TO ATTRACT WEALTH

There are many different types of wealth. This fragrant spell asks you to consider what real wealth means to you as you invite it into your life.

You will need:

piece of amber
oud essential oil
3 gold candles
pen or pencil and paper

1. On the evening of a Full Moon, place the piece of amber on your sacred altar or table. Drip three drops of oud onto the amber, before placing the candles in a triangle around it and lighting each candle.
2. Now drip one drop of oud oil onto the back of your hand and gently wave it in the air. (If you have sensitive skin or are prone to allergies, be sure to dilute the oil in a small amount of water first.) As you inhale, be aware of how the sensual warmth of the musty wood fragrance diffuses through the air.
3. Focus on the candles for a moment and repeat the following charm:

    'Upon a tree in far off places
    There is a trick to bring us riches –
    A riot, a malady of Earth

Which tricks the bark and turns to mirth.
This fungal gold is wildly bold,
Its fragrance pungent like a toad,
Yet deep, exotic, dark and rude
Its perfumed jewel is precious oud.'

4. Now copy down the verse onto the piece of paper.
5. Finally, on the same piece of paper, write down the kind of wealth you are seeking. Fold the paper, blow out the candles and place the amber on top of the paper for one lunar cycle to attract and manifest your chosen type of wealth.

Thyme

Magic tradition: Celtic and European
Sacred meaning: courage, strength, positive attitude and plentiful ideas

A member of the mint family, this low-growing herb's name derives either from the Greek *thuo* (meaning 'I sacrifice'), or *thumos* ('courage'). Its powerful smell revives the spirits; the Roman writer and naturalist Pliny the Elder said that when burned, wild thyme would 'put to flight all creeping venomous creatures'. In medieval Europe, thyme was a favoured herb for love charms, while in Christian folklore it was thought to be part of the bedding used by the Virgin Mary for the birth of Jesus. As a medicinal herb, thyme has been used for centuries to help ease anxiety, and in aromatherapy it's thought to restore courage and to ignite the spirit of adventure. To bring a sense of reward, excitement and optimism into our lives, thyme can be grown freely in the garden or in pots placed on a sunny window ledge.

CHARM FOR ABUNDANCE

The more you are positive about yourself and your future, the more abundance will come into your life – whatever it is that you seek.

You will need:

a generous handful of fresh thyme (or a pouch filled with dried thyme)

1. If possible, stand in an open place that is situated on a hill or mountain, and which is far from tall trees, buildings, electricity cables, beacons and so on. The more engaged you can be with the openness of nature around you, the better.
2. Hold the thyme in your hand and turn to face north. Open your hand and blow some of the thyme in that direction. Repeat this process three times, turning clockwise to the east, south and west.
3. Each time you blow away the thyme, strongly visualise what kind of abundance you are seeking and verbalise your desire.

4. Return home, and you will be blessed with abundance in the weeks to come.

Wild garlic

Magic tradition: Wicca, Celtic, Chinese, Hindu and Egyptian
Sacred meaning: protection, actualising, manifestation and plenty

Renowned in European folklore as a plant that repels vampires, and in Cuba as a safeguard against jaundice, garlic is a global culinary ingredient that has been associated with a wide range of superstitions and powers over the centuries. Cultivated over four thousand years ago in ancient Mesopotamia, well-preserved garlic was also found in the tomb of Tutankhamun dating from around 1325 BCE. In Chinese and European folk traditions, garlic has long been associated with witchcraft and was hung in the home to deter evil spirits or demons. In ancient Greek folk magic, garlic was placed at crossroads as an offering to the goddess Hecate so that she might bestow her favour. In medieval Bologna in Italy, it was considered a symbol of plenty and buried on midsummer night as a charm against poverty. In addition to its use as a powerful flavouring and garnish, garlic has also been known for its antiseptic properties and as a cardiovascular cleanser. In magic, it can be used to repel negativity and attract blessings.

Charm to Manifest a Goal

Use this fragrant charm to attract good luck and support your efforts towards achieving a realistic goal.

You will need:

2-metre (6.5-foot) length of gold ribbon or thread
a bunch of parsley
3 green olives
5 wild garlic flowers (or garlic cloves)
3 comfrey leaves
1 piece of aquamarine
bowl

1. Make five equidistant knots along your gold ribbon or thread.
2. Place all the other ingredients in the bowl in any random order (your choice defines your personal connection to the universe). Now wind the golden thread round and round in an anticlockwise spiral on top of the contents in the bowl.
3. As you do so, repeat this charm:

   'Take peppered olives, parsley green,
   Wild garlic flowers and aquamarine,
   Five knots along a golden thread,
   Take leaves of comfrey, so it's said,
   Work now this well and make a brew
   To manifest a goal for you.'

4. Leave your offering overnight and then recycle the herbs as appropriate. Keep the aquamarine in a safe place, and within one lunar cycle you will be well on your way to manifesting your goal.

Fauna

Squirrel

Magic tradition: North America, Europe and Asia
Sacred meaning: accumulating, saving, planning, being goal-oriented and agile

The ubiquitous squirrel is a symbol of mischievous energy worldwide. In Native American folklore, squirrels often spread gossip, instigate trouble and annoy others with their antics. In some stories, they are praised for their wise foraging or are honoured spirits as caretakers of the forest. To the Choctaw people of south-east America, the black squirrel was responsible for the eclipse of the Sun as it gnawed away at the solar disc in the sky. In Norse myth, Ratatoskr was a squirrel who raced around Yggdrasil, the world tree, carrying insulting messages between a wise eagle perched on top of the tree and Níðhöggr, the serpent who lived beneath the tree's roots. In magic work, the squirrel represents planning for the future, in order to be one step ahead of the game.

PRACTICE TO ENSURE FUTURE PROSPERITY

To ensure your future will be filled with plenty – whether for your own security, financial support or just a feeling of enrichment and material abundance – you're going to be a bit of a squirrel.

You will need:

> pouch or paper bag filled with wild nuts (foraged nuts would be ideal)
> a lovely tree
> fork or trowel

1. First, gather your nuts in the bag, grab your trowel and set off to the tree of your choice.
2. At the base of your chosen tree, begin to bury your nuts. Use the trowel if needed, but do so without disturbing the tree's roots. Bury one nut at a time in a circle, working in a clockwise direction until you have totally surrounded the tree.
3. As you bury each nut, say, 'With this nut I care for Mother Nature, and she in turn will bring me security.'
4. Leave your squirrel treasure trove and your future security will be assured.

Toad

Magic tradition: China, Asia, Europe and
Native American
Sacred meaning: protecting wealth, attracting money
and material security

The Money Toad or Jin Chan is a popular symbol in the
Chinese art of feng shui, as it's believed to attract and protect wealth and to guard against bad luck. Ancient Chinese
legends also refer to the toad's secret of immortality. In
one story, a wandering wise man called Liu Hai befriended
a three-legged toad, Ch'an Chu. As a reward for being a
loyal friend, the toad revealed his secret of eternal life to
the wise man. In Native American culture, an Iroquois
myth describes how a toad helped create the world with
mud. Roman naturalist and writer Pliny the Elder believed
that a toad's presence would silence a room full of people
and that a magical jewel known as the 'toadstone' could be
found inside a toad's head. Toadstones are actually bufonite, the button-shaped fossilised teeth of a prehistoric fish
found in rock formations. During the medieval period, it
was believed that if the magical toadstone were crafted
into a ring, it could protect its wearer, as the stone would
change colour in the presence of poison. However, during
the witchhunts throughout Europe, toads were viewed as
evil and thought to be witches' familiars.

TOAD SPELL TO ATTRACT MONEY

This simple spell will bring you money, as long as you make it clear exactly how much money you truly need. (No gold-diggers!) There's no point being unrealistic either, as the universe won't oblige those who have no true sense of worth or value. Instead, this charm can help you to feel secure and receive the amount you need to nurture your well-being. (If you can't obtain toadstones, i.e. bufonite, you can substitute them with five brown or black polished obsidian stones.)

You will need:

1 white candle
1 black candle
pen or pencil and paper
5 polished toadstones

1. On the evening of a Waxing Moon, place the candles side by side on your sacred altar or a table and then light them.
2. Next, take your paper and draw a pentagram talisman. In the middle section of the star, write down exactly how much money you require.
3. Now, place a toadstone on each of the five points, repeating the following incantation as you do so:

   'With black and white
   And toadstones bright,

Their luck to sing
My wealth to bring.'

4. Blow out the candles and leave your offering to the universe until the Full Moon. You will soon receive the money you truly deserve.

Landscape

Volcano

Magic tradition: Icelandic, Southeast Asia, Southern Europe, Māori and Polynesia
Sacred meaning: passion, explosive energy, excitement and inspiration

Wherever there are volcanoes in the world, there is sure to be a local presiding deity and legend among indigenous peoples. For example, in Hawaii, Pele was the jealous and passionate goddess of volcanoes and fire; in Māori mythology, Rūaumoko, the god of earthquakes, volcanoes and seasons, was the son of the sky father and Earth mother known as Rangi and Papa. The fire and volcano god in Roman mythology was Vulcan, and the Bicolano god of fire, Gugarang, was thought to live inside Mount Mayon, an active volcano in the Philippines. In Iceland, the Hekla volcano was believed to be a gateway to hell, while the Katla volcano was regarded as the home of a vengeful sorceress. When they erupt, volcanoes explode with tremendous energy and power, while volcanic soil can be a source of abundance.

Spell for Abundant Inspiration

Abundance isn't just about material wealth; it's also about the richness of the mind, new ideas, exciting plans and projects. This spell will enable you to profit from the explosive nature of the volcano, which will shower you with fiery ideas and empower creativity. Make sure to take extra care, as you will be picking up the central candle when it is lit.

You will need:

needle or pin
1 red taper candle (in a candlestick)
2 red tea-light candles

1. Using the needle or pin, engrave the following vertically down one side of the red taper candle: 'I burn the fire to see the flame'.
2. On the other side of the candle, engrave vertically: 'I see the flame to fire my name'.
3. Place the two tea-light candles either side of the red candle.
4. Light your three candles and gaze into the flames for a few minutes to find stillness and connection to the energy of fire.

5. Carefully take the red taper candle and, holding it at a slight angle, let one drop of wax drip onto the tea-light candle to the left, and then repeat the same action to the tea-light candle on the right. Let the flames burn for a few more minutes before you blow them all out, and you will have sealed your intention for volcanic, passionate inspiration.

Mist and fog

Magic tradition: wherever they occur
Sacred meaning: confusion, lack of vision, revision and reawakening

Although technically this is about the weather, the land-scape itself is often obscured or blanketed by swirling mists and fog. This can create an atmosphere of fear, a sense of being lost and of losing direction, or a feeling that you are stumbling blindly along a pathway. We associate mists with Gothic novels, witchcraft and evil spirits, and we imagine phantoms, vague shapes and creepy beings; or maybe we even see into other worlds? Mist can represent a lack of self-belief when our sense of clarity is fogged up by problems or the demanding egos of others – which is when the next spell can be very helpful.

SPELL TO CLEAR AWAY THE MIST
FOR PROSPEROUS IDEAS

To clear the air and to make way for sunshiny, prosperous days ahead, perform this practice to honour the mist, knowing it will soon disperse to reveal a bright, sunny day and a sense of reawakening. If you have the chance to walk through mist or fog during this spell, then so much the better. If you don't, then close your eyes and imagine you are in the middle of a thick fog and have lost your way completely.

1. Stand in the mist or fog and be aware of the stillness, how sounds are muffled or distorted, how damp the air feels and how vague and indistinct the landscape looks.

2. Reach your arms out in front of you and begin to move your hands in circles, as if you were massaging a horse. Continue for twenty seconds or so, then repeat in the opposite direction. Can you feel the air move? The water particles touching your hands? Is the mist actually as real as you are? If so, then it too has a part to play in nature and its very obscurity is the pathway to seeing the light.

3. Make your way out of the mist when you can, or wait for it to clear away, and with a flash of insight, you will see clearly how to make your future a prosperous one. If you are using your imagination for this practice, open your eyes and see the sunny day, and how the mist has cleared

away to give you a new perspective on life. Now you are ready to engage in prosperous ideas with self-determination.

Sky and stars

Shooting star

Magic tradition: worldwide
Sacred meaning: good luck, bounty, success and wish-fulfilment

When meteoroids – fragments of rock and dust made up of iron and/or silica – pass through the Earth's atmosphere, the particles burn up to produce brilliant streaks of light that can be seen around the world in the night sky. These short-lived, spectacular trails of light are known as meteors or shooting stars. Meteor showers, when there are seemingly hundreds of shooting stars, are caused when the Earth passes through the trail of debris left by a comet. The well-known meteor shower the Perseids can usually be seen in early August and is named after the constellation Perseus. In mythology, Perseus was the son of the Greek god Zeus. He was conceived when Zeus came to the mortal princess Danae disguised as a shower of gold. It is believed in most magic traditions that if you see a shooting star you will enjoy good luck, and if you repeat the word 'money' three times before the light burns out, you'll quickly attract money to yourself.

WISH UPON A STAR FOR LUCK

This charm will bring you glorious showers of good luck in your material and financial endeavours. Make sure you attempt it somewhere quiet, where you won't be distracted by other people. Researching when and where certain meteor showers are likely to fall will be incredibly helpful with the timing.

You will need:

>   patience
>   timing
>   a shooting star
>   a wish

1. Quite simply, if you are prepared to spend a few hours gazing up at the night sky at certain times of the year, and there is no light pollution and you have a wide, open vista of heavens before you, then the chances are you will spot a falling star.

2. The magic of this shooting star charm can only be achieved by seeing the real thing. So when you do spot your star, either make your wish, or say, 'Money, money, money', before the starlight burns away – and you will be rewarded by the universe with your desire.

3. If you really can't get into nature to see the real thing, then every time you can physically gaze up at the night sky, look to the stars and send out

positive blessings, and the universe will look after you as best it can.

Lightning

Magic tradition: worldwide
Sacred meaning: illumination, new perspective, end of outdated assumptions and breakthrough

Lightning is a powerful discharge of high-voltage electricity between a cloud and the ground, creating bright flashes and resulting thunder (see page 213 for more on thunder). Fork lightning, the most spectacular kind to see, is when a build-up of positive charge forms on the ground beneath the cloud, and is attracted to and connects with the negative charge at the bottom of the cloud, thereby creating cloud-to-ground lightning. To the Navajo Indians, lightning was a wink in the spirit Thunderbird's eye and an important aspect of healing rituals and crop growth. In Greek mythology, Zeus tossed thunderbolts when angered, and any tree struck by lightning was regarded as sacred. In Aboriginal tradition, Namarrkon is the lightning man who rides a storm cloud and throws lightning bolts at humans and trees. He soaks up the Sun's rays, which form bright arcs of light across each of his shoulders. According to a medieval superstition first noted by a ninth-century French bishop, weather witches or *tempestarii* were believed to be in league with a mythical race of cloud-dwellers who sent lightning storms to cause havoc on Earth. Lightning is dangerous, so please don't go out in a storm; instead, stay safely indoors. Even though it calls on lightning, you can practise the following spell on a day when the weather is calm.

FINANCIAL BREAKTHROUGH SPELL

If you are hoping for a financial breakthrough of some kind, perhaps to help further your plans or enable you to start anew, this spell can help support your wishes.

You will need:

forked stick or forked fallen branch

1. Take your stick or branch and find a quiet place outdoors, where you won't be distracted. (But please make sure you don't try this practice outside during a storm.)
2. First, call in the four directions to aid you. Turn to face the north and point the fork of your stick in that direction and say: 'Wind to the north, come lighten my world.' Then repeat by facing and summoning the winds of the east, the south and the west.
3. Next, trace a magic circle on the ground with your forked stick, moving in an anticlockwise direction. Stand in stillness for a minute with the forked stick pointing to the ground. Now turn the stick the other way and point the fork up to the sky.

4. Repeat the following enchantment: 'With rod empowered, this lightning fork connection will send me all I need to start afresh, or bring financial benefits from this moment. Blessings to the powers of nature.'

5. Hold the stick up to the sky for a few moments to charge the energy between you and the sky. Then, when you have finished the ritual, keep your lightning rod in a safe place with the fork always pointing to the sky. All being well, you will soon enjoy the financial breakthrough that you have been seeking.

Chapter 15

Creativity, Spiritual Growth and Inner Magic

Throughout this book, we have looked at ways to practise Earth magic so that it benefits the Earth and nature, as well as ourselves. This final chapter is devoted to bestowing not only ourselves but the entire planet and all who live on it with healing spiritual or creative energy, so that we can all share in the calm of life and the joy of being at one.

Flora

Jasmine

Magic tradition: Hindu, Oceanian and European
Sacred meaning: spiritual love, purity, happiness and attraction

Native to the tropical and temperate regions of Oceania and Eurasia, this highly fragrant flower is prized in the perfume and essential-oil industries. Its aroma is also used in tea. The name jasmine originates in an ancient Persian word meaning 'gift from God', and jasmine oil has traditionally been used for invoking physical love. Another headily perfumed jasmine-type flower known as night jasmine, or Parijat (*Nyctanthes arbor-tristis*), is indigenous to India and south-east Asia. Because its petals lose their fragrance and fall during the day, this plant is known as 'the tree of sorrow'. Parijat is used in Ayurvedic medicine and is central to the myth of the Sun god Sura and his love for the mortal princess Parijat. Whenever Sura tried to visit Parijat, his solar rays threatened to burn her up, so the gods turned her into a tree. From then on, Sura visited her at night when her fragrant flowers bloomed to welcome him in the darkness. Jasmine is also associated with the Greek goddess Aphrodite, and is believed to attract love, lust and happiness when worn as a perfume or woven into garlands or bouquets. Jasmine is thought to enhance all forms of spiritual healing as well.

JASMINE SPELL FOR SPIRITUAL WELL-BEING

This is a beautifully soothing spell to do on a warm summer's evening, when jasmine will be in full flower and at its most fragrant.

You will need:

a pin or needle
1 white candle
a handful of jasmine flowers
jasmine essential oil

1. On the evening of a Waxing Moon, take the pin or needle and use it to inscribe your name into the wax of the candle. Place the candle on your sacred altar or a table, light it, and then place the handful of flowers in front of it.

2. Drip one drop of essential oil on the candle (making sure to avoid the flame), one drop on each of your wrists (if you have sensitive skin or are prone to allergies, be sure to dilute the oil in a small amount of water first), and one drop on the flowers. Breathe in the fragrance and imagine you are connected to the spirit and soul of the universe. Focus on the smell and be mindful of how it makes you feel. Then imagine it permeating every pore of your body, filling you with spiritual light, until you are connected to the pure energy of the universe.

Come out of your meditation when you are ready and blow out the candle. You will feel inspired, pure, happy and calm. You can repeat this simple spell whenever jasmine is in flower and you feel that your spiritual well-being is in need of a boost.

Water lily

Magic tradition: Asia, Europe, Australasia, Oceania and the Americas
Sacred meaning: creativity, hope, rebirth, wellness and spiritual growth

This aquatic plant has floating leaves with long, rope-like rhizomes or stems. Its Latin name, *Nymphaea*, is rooted in the Greek 'nymphs', the name of those spirits found in wells, springs, streams and other waterways. In ancient Egypt, the white water lily (*Nymphaea lotus*) and the blue Egyptian water lily (*Nymphaea caerulea*) both became symbolic of the Upper Nile as the creator of all life. The flowers of the blue Egyptian water lily open in the morning and then sink beneath the water at dusk; while those of the white water lily open at night and close in the morning. In Native American mythology, one folk legend tells of how a moonbeam sprite became trapped on Earth and fell in love with the Dakota chief's son. As they rowed across a treacherous lake to receive the chief's marriage blessing, the sprite tragically drowned, and the next day the first ever yellow water lily bloomed from the spot in the lake. Similarly, like the lotus, the water lily takes root in the mud at the bottom of a pond or lake, growing out of it to become the most beautiful flower on the water's surface — a magnificent symbol of our own spiritual growth.

WATER LILY SPELL TO INVOKE SPIRITUAL GROWTH

This spell can help to connect you to your spiritual self and offer a moment of welcome calm. If you can, do it while sitting next to a pond or water where water lilies grow. If this isn't possible, use your favourite image of water lilies and a clear bowl of water as a substitute.

You will need:

5 lotus seeds

1. If you are lucky enough to be able to sit beside a real water lily pond, relax and focus on a flower or even just a floating leaf. If you are using a bowl of water, place it on the image of your pond and gaze into the bowl.
2. Next, you want to gently throw the lotus seeds, one at a time, into the pond or bowl, repeating the following incantation with each seed:

    'From the pond of life there grows a seed
    Of understanding, less of need,

As stillness quakes and dragons fly
There like a lily flower we rise.'

3. Thank the water lily for its power to connect you to your spiritual self and for nurturing your belief in nature's magic.

Fauna

Hummingbird

Magic tradition: Aztec, Equatorial, South America, North America and Caribbean
Sacred meaning: joy, accomplishment, creativity, enchantment and imagination

Blessed with brightly coloured, iridescent feathers and the unique ability to fly in any direction, including backwards, the hummingbird flutters its wings at up to an incredible eighty beats per second. Nicknamed 'Flying Jewels', they hover in mid-air when sipping nectar with their long, slender beaks and are thought to visit over a thousand flowers a day. The hyper-busy hummingbird is also a bit of a thief and steals insects that are trapped in spider webs, sometimes using the fine threads to weave their own nests too. In Aztec mythology, the hummingbird represents the powerful Sun god Huitzilopochtli, conceived by his mother after she clutched a ball of hummingbird feathers to her breasts. The Native American

Indians believed this bird to be a symbol of luck, devotion, permanence and the cycle of life. The Cherokee believed shamans adopted the form of a hummingbird in order to visit the spirit world to find healing plants. The hummingbird is associated with rebirth, dreams, creativity and a joyful spirit, and its feathers were once used by the ancient Mayan peoples in love spells. As a totem spirit bird, the hummingbird will bring you joy, achievement and creative empowerment.

HUMMINGBIRD POTION FOR CREATIVITY AND JOY

Hummingbirds love colour and sweet nectar, and can help you to bring colour and the sweetness of creativity and joy into your life too.

You will need:

1 pot of honey
long-handled spoon or a chopstick

1. Sit in a comfortable position with a pot of honey and your spoon or chopstick before you. Dip your utensil into the honey, close your eyes and taste the honey.
2. Think about how sweet but how natural the honey tastes. Imagine or pretend you are a hummingbird: how fast would you beat your wings to make

your humming sound? How would you sing? How would you fly, jewel-like, through the sky?

3. Repeat the following incantation as you slowly stir the honey in a clockwise direction with your utensil:

> *'A potion brewed of nectar's honey*
> *Brings hummingbirds so fast, so lovely,*
> *When down the pot of ignorance*
> *We find there is some recompense*
> *With sweetest waters of desire*
> *When hummingbirds have wings of fire.'*

4. Place the utensil against your lips and take a taste if you so desire, and thank the hummingbird for giving you creative joy. Store your honeypot in your witch's cupboard and if you ever need a boost of creative joy repeat the spell.

Domestic cat

Magic tradition: worldwide
Sacred meaning: guardianship, detachment, sensuality, mystery, magic, independence, wisdom and vigilance

The domestic cat succeeds in guarding its mystery and independence to such a degree that some people hate cats while others adore the fact that cats only let us love them when they choose! Our feline friends are indispensable in magic, embodying an instinctive, ancient power that comes from their association with Egyptian deities such as Bastet, Sekhmet and Mut. If you don't know a domestic cat, or aren't lucky enough to have been chosen as their 'familiar' or friend, it's time to connect to their mysterious nature, and thereby get a better understanding of the depths of your own wisdom.

CAT CHARM FOR CONNECTION TO THE WISDOM OF THE UNIVERSE

This charm will help you to open up your spirit and soul to your hidden inner magic, as subtle and as wise as the cat's.

You will need:

1 red candle
1 tiger's eye crystal

1. Place the candle on your sacred altar or a table, with the tiger's eye next to it.
2. Sit in a relaxed position on the floor and repeat the following affirmation: 'With tiger's eye, I am ready to become aligned to the magic of the cat.'
3. Then lay flat on your back and stretch from fingertips to toes, imagining that you are a cat stretching. Take your time, luxuriate in the feeling of the stretch, and stay there for 30 to 60 seconds.
4. When you are ready, slowly stand up and face each

of the four directions. First face the north, then the east, then the south and finally the west and repeat each time the following affirmation: 'With feline essence, I become at one with the universe and all that is my inner mystery, to help me achieve great wisdom.'

5. Blow out the candle and take up the tiger's eye. Carry or wear it for one lunar cycle to open your spirit and soul to your inner magic.

Fox

Magic tradition: Northern Hemisphere and parts of North Africa
Sacred meaning: cunning, agility, quick-wittedness, master planner, independent, powers of shape-shifting and invisibility

Vulpes vulpes, commonly known as the red fox, is renowned for its ability to adapt and survive in urban areas, and is now indigenous to many big cities. Throughout myth and folklore, the fox has a reputation for cunning, shape-shifting and other magical powers. In Mesopotamian mythology, the fox is one of the sacred animals of the goddess Ninhursag, acting as her messenger. In Chinese, Japanese and south-east Asian folklore, fox spirits – known as *huli jing* in China, *kitsune* in Japan and *kumiho* in Korea – are mischievous, cunning shape-shifters, who transform into beautiful women to seduce men and rob them of their masculinity or power (a common feature of shape-shifting spirits in the East). In one Finnish myth, the fox is said to conjure the aurora borealis while it runs through the snow. As its fur brushes against the snow, it creates magical sparks and sets the sky ablaze. Even today, the Finnish word for the aurora is *revontulet*, translating as 'fox fires'.

FOX CEREMONY TO BOOST CREATIVE PLANNING

To bring to life your imagination, clear your mind of clutter, and be filled with insight, persistence, silent determination, and the ability to be a master-planner, celebrate the essence of the fox by inviting its spirit guide to come to you.

You will need:

1 yellow candle
image of a fox
piece of citrine

1. Place the candle on your sacred altar or on a table and light it. Then place the image of your fox in front of it and put the citrine on top of the image. Sit quietly and focus on the candle flame for a few minutes.
2. Now take up the citrine in your hand and repeat the following: 'To the spirit fox, I welcome you

into my life, so guide me in all ways to master my own destiny. Bring me imagination, insight and determination, and show me the way.'

3. Stay still for a few minutes before replacing the citrine on the image. Then say: 'I affirm the fox as my guiding spirit.'

4. You are now ready to stay connected to the fox, so take up the citrine again and place it in your pocket or bag. Take it with you wherever you go to draw helpful mentors to yourself and so that the fox spirit can guide you in all your creative plans.

Sky and stars

Rain

Magic tradition: worldwide
Sacred meaning: fertility, growth, relief and creative ability

From the Navajo people's god of rain, Neinilli, to the Vedic deity Parjanya, most ancient peoples believed the weather to be caused by divine forces. Worshipping or making offerings to the gods would ensure the rains would fall and subsequently improve Earth's fertility. Of course, rain is not always welcome, so in magic there were also spells to prevent floods and storms. Native American peoples prayed to the ancestors for gentle rains when planting, but in Polynesian folklore, ritual drumming was performed under the Full Moon to prevent hurricanes and storms. Medieval monks observed how a hazel stick flowed downstream: if at the dead centre of the stream, it was a sign to harvest the hops straight away before the autumn rains arrived. If the stick meandered or stayed close to the bank, then they could wait until the next New Moon. (Even monks believed in folklore, especially when it came to brewing their own beer!) Weather witches, shamans and sorcerers worldwide were once in demand for their ability to predict and, more importantly, influence the weather. In ancient Egypt, magicians used spells to raise winds and storms against enemy invaders. In medieval Europe, witches were said to conjure up rain by a range of means, such as casting pieces of flint behind their backs, flinging sand into the air, or striking a river with a broom so the water would rise up to the sky and fall down as magical rain.

Being at One with the Rain for Creative Power

This spell will enable you to benefit from being at one with the nourishing, fertilising aspects of rain and to invoke your creative power. If you are living in a location where it is very unlikely to rain for some time, perform the following spell twice, once at the New Crescent Moon and once at the Full Moon.

You will need:

1 white quartz crystal
jug of spring water, naturally sourced water or
    recent rainfall (optional)
sieve (optional)

1. It is best to do this spell on a rainy day at the New Crescent Moon if you can. Go outside and stand in the rain, and place your crystal on the ground, letting the rain fall onto it. If you can't stand out in the rain, place your piece of quartz on a surface that can get wet, and gradually pour a jug of water through a sieve so it rains over the crystal.

2. As the rain or water falls, repeat:

   'Rain, it comes to bring me power;
   Rain, it comes to bring me growth;
   Rain, it comes with creative joy!'

3. As the rain pours over you, or water falls on the quartz, feel it washing you with creative energy, mirroring your purification of the white quartz.

4. Take up the crystal and keep it on your desk, work space or wherever you want to get creative, and it will imbue you with the spirit of the rain.

Autumnal equinox

Magic tradition: worldwide
Sacred meaning: completion, harvest, gratitude, sharing and reaping rewards

The spring and autumnal equinoxes mark two astronomical moments in the year when the Sun is positioned exactly above the celestial equator, and day and night are of equal length. In the Northern Hemisphere, the autumnal equinox occurs around 22 September, and in the Southern Hemisphere the autumnal equinox occurs around 21 March. The autumnal equinox also marks the middle of the harvest season. Traditionally, this is the time of festivals, such as the Neopagan festival of Mabon, named after the Welsh god of light. In many pagan and Wiccan traditions, this is a time of giving thanks for the things we have, whether this is abundant crops, happy relationships or being at peace with nature. It's a time of plenty, gratitude and sharing.

Autumn Equinox Ritual

To harvest your own creativity, give gratitude to Mother Earth by performing the following ritual at the autumn equinox.

You will need:

selection of fruit and leaves of apples, sloes,
    elderberries, blackberries or hawthorn
    berries, or any other autumnal fruits or
    berries native to your local region
cedarwood essential oil
vervain essential oil

1. Make an outdoor altar to give thanks to nature's
    abundance. Leave a selection of your fruit and
    leaves as a gift.
2. Cut one apple in half, widthways, to reveal the
    five-pointed star made by the seeds. This corres-
    ponds to the five elements of Earth, Air, Fire,
    Water and Spirit.
3. Repeat the following spell as you hold the apple in
    your hand (and then write it down in your journal
    as part of the ceremony):

'The harvest came and took the sheaf
Of Mother Nature's perfect wreath —
Of berries, aconites or rue,
The song of summer over too.
Take now the elder, blow the down
Of dandelion and princes found,
Of birch trees silken in the night,
Till all who know put love to right,
Of wrongs of those whose path is lain,
With cedarwood and cool vervain,

> *Untie the knot and bind your heart*
> *With Water, Earth, Air, Fire and Spirit's part.'*

4. Remove the seeds and place them on your altar, then eat as much as you want of the apple – and you will soon be harvesting and reaping rewards of your own creativity.

Landscape

Shades and shadows

Magic tradition: wherever shadow falls
Sacred meaning: soul, the unconscious, guiding daemon and self-protection

The landscape is filled with shadows and shaded places if we care to look. However, throughout world folklore, shadows are often associated with malevolent energy, underworlds, demons and black magic. Shadow people come to taunt or scare us in our sleep, or lurk as strange black shapes in our peripheral vision. In Greek mythology, Erebus was a primordial deity and the personification of darkness and shadows. With his sister Nyx, the goddess of the night, he parented the fearsome Nemesis, goddess of divine retribution, and the Moirai, the three goddesses of destiny, known as the Fates. In European superstition, it was believed that if someone did not have a shadow, then they had no soul. But shadows do have positive benefits. Standing in the shade or in the shadow of a great tree can protect us from the glare of the Sun. Shadows can also help us to establish the time and our location: the length and direction of a shadow on the ground or on a sundial can tell us what time it is and even where we are in the world, depending on the angle of the shadow. Some plants thrive in the shade, as do many medicinal plants, wild fungi and rare species. The nineteenth-century Romantic English poet Wordsworth wrote:

> 'The daisy, by the shadow that it casts,
> Protects the lingering dew-drop from the sun.'

Similarly, the following magic charm will help to align you with Earth's shadow places for the protection they can offer.

SHADOW PROTECTION SPELL

This spell works with shadows as a way to connect with Mother Nature's protective powers. Make sure to attempt it only on a sunny day, but avoid midday in the summer as little shadow will be cast.

You will need:

access to a large, shady tree
1 stick about 60 centimetres (2 foot) long
cup of chamomile tea
your journal or Book of Shadows

1. Find a large, shady tree, take your stick and fix it into the ground beyond the tree's shade so that the stick casts its own shadow.

2. Sit beneath the tree in the shade. If you stay there for at least ten minutes, sipping your tea, you will begin to see the shadow change. It will grow longer or shorter depending on the time of day.

3. As you sip your calming tea, write down the following spell in your journal or Book of Shadows:

   'This charm, it shows you how to go
   To shadowed places you don't know,
   With crystals red or precious jewels —
   Take one of green and one of blue.
   And never show your will is done
   Or all your work will be undone.
   Take lamium, and potent oud,
   Reverse the spell and make a brew
   Of chamomile and rosemary fair,
   Twist canes of bryony in your hair.
   This potion scattered all around
   Will bring the Dryads and their sounds
   Of night-time owls and moonlit glades
   Where now you languish in the shade.
   Your work is done, the spell is cast —
   Drink now the potion, all will pass.'

4. When you have finished writing, perhaps sketch some flowers around the verse, or add some symbols that mean something significant to you.

5. See how the shadow of your stick has moved, and how you are protected by the shade. From now, you will on be protected by Mother Nature's spiritual shadows after drinking your magical tea.

Ocean

We return one more time to the ocean, simply because it is one of the most empowering symbols of landscape in the world. It is the ultimate symbol of spiritual connection and will enable you to enjoy a close relationship with the Soul of the World.

OCEAN AFFIRMATION

This ocean affirmation will need to be carried out by the seashore, so try it the next time you visit a beach.

You will need:

   12 sea shells
   illustration of the 12 zodiac symbols
   indelible ink or paint

1. Draw or paint a zodiac symbol on each shell with an indelible medium. The twelves signs of the zodiac symbolise the twelve aspects of yourself in your horoscope – the qualities and potentials you possess that will be important to you throughout your journey through life.

2. Place the shells in your pocket and stand on the seashore for a while, focusing on the far-away horizon.

3. To affirm your intention to create a close spiritual connection with planet Earth, repeat this simple affirmation: 'My spirit and soul, my heart and mind will be entwined with the soul of the world.'

4. Now, walk along the beach and bury one shell at a time wherever you feel a patch of beach speaks to you. In this way, you are symbolically leaving your spiritual footprint with each shell you bury. When the tide comes in, your shells may be washed away and carried to other parts of the beach or into the ocean to spread your affirmation to the world.

Sacred places

Ancient monuments

Magic tradition: worldwide
Sacred meaning: blessing, divine connection and spiritual energy

If you live near to a sacred monument or place, then do visit it and perform this little salutation in person. If that's not possible, look online for a sacred site that attracts you. It could be Celtic standing stones, an ancient burial chamber, the Pyramids, Knossos, an Irish earthwork, a Hindu, Buddhist or Incan temple, a Native American Medicine

Wheel, or whatever else you like the look of. This place is there to bring you closer to the divine that flows through all of nature, which is often intensified with a powerful presence in these silent sites. Such places are frequently associated with a vortex of spiralling energy that connects us to the universe, so you are going to engage with that energy now.

1. At your chosen location or in your home, stand or sit for a while and take in the essence of the place. Focus on what makes it special. Does it exude spiritual or divine energy? Do you sense ancient spiritual footprints of those who have passed through, or is it a gateway to another world? All you need to do is focus on your chosen place or image, or find stillness and calm in the site you have chosen.

2. Now sit cross-legged if you wish, close your eyes, rest your hands on your knees with your palms turned upwards and feel your sitting bones rooted to the floor. Open your mind, body and soul to the energy you feel around you. The more solitary you are the better, so take your time and be inspired afterwards to write a note in your journal about how you felt.

3. To invoke this feeling of divine connection, return here whenever you can, either in your imagination or in reality. If you have the chance to visit other sacred monuments, then you will begin to find a connection between them all; a

sense of connecting, in fact, to the magic of the world itself, which is the divine energy that flows through everything.

The guardian witch – you

The most sacred place on Earth is you. And the more you believe in your connection to the Earth and that you have become a guardian witch, the more you will be able to make magic work for you.

SPELL TO CONNECT WITH THE GUARDIAN WITCH WITHIN

Whenever you feel in need of comfort, spiritual blessing or simply to feel engaged with this sacred side of yourself, perform the following magical practice:

You will need:

1 white candle
mirror
pen or pencil
your journal or Book of Shadows

1. Sit or stand in front of the mirror and light the candle. For a few minutes gaze at your reflection and enjoy what you see there. Focus on the candle flame too, and you may even see into the magic of nature itself if you are close enough.

2. Write the following spell in your journal and then say it out loud. As you do so, remember this is you – the guardian witch who is now ready to make life what you want it to be:

'Such jewels she has upon her hand,
A diamond here, a glittering band;
And there she holds out other stones
Of red agate, or crimson bones.
Beneath her crown she carries gold,
Of foils and rubies, emeralds too.
But mostly spun in lunar threads,
Her dress is wove from ocean beds.
And so her song is one of joy
Of lullabies that reach the sky
Where high above blue mantles clear
The Guardian Witch – you'll find her here.'

3. You are now deeply connected with your own magic within and to the sacred world around you.

Conclusion

The early twentieth-century mystic, artist and poet Khalil Gibran wrote, 'Forget not that the Earth delights to feel your bare feet and the winds long to play with your hair.' It is in this spirit, and the one in which this book was written, that I ask you to remember that the world out there – and Mother Earth herself – notices you, touches you, caresses and nurtures you. But only if you will let her and embrace her in return too.

This book is about opening your mind, soul and spirit to nature, Earth, the universe and inviting these into your life. You can make magic for yourself and those you love – and give back to nature your trust.

I hope you will let the Earth delight in you.

Glossary of Correspondences

Here you will find suggested ingredients and other sacred resources for use in your magic work – some are required for the spells in this book, while others can be used to create your own rituals and charms. It's also important to stress that working with deities and invoking their help to connect to the spiritual world around you is a crucial aspect of magic work. If you are unfamiliar with the deities referenced in this book, why not take some time to research and appreciate their spiritual traditions.

This glossary has been categorised by theme to make it as user-friendly as possible. For example, if you are in need of abundant ideas, you would choose ingredients in the associated list: you might set up a meditation altar in your sacred garden and ask the Hindu god, Ganesha, for positive thoughts and good luck; you could light a red candle, place a piece of malachite before the candle and drop a little patchouli oil on the crystal while repeating a charm. If you wish, you can also mix and match ingredients to reinforce various elements of your ritual or charm. But most of all, take pleasure and delight in the resources that Mother Nature offers you with open arms.

Love and relationships

Deities to invoke for love and relationships
Áine (Celtic)
Aphrodite (Greek)
Eros (Greek)
Freyja (Norse)
Hathor (Egyptian)
Inanna (Sumerian)
Rati (Hindu)
Venus (Roman)

Botanicals for love and relationships
basil
hawthorn
jasmine
lavender
lily
lemon verbena
orchid
rose
rosemary
wormwood

Colours for love and relationships
pink (romance, attraction)
red (passion, sexuality)
white (purity, commitment)
yellow (friendship)

Crystals and precious stones for love and relationships

    emerald
    garnet
    kunzite
    lepidolite
    red carnelian
    red jasper
    rose quartz crystal
    ruby

Essential oils for love and relationships

    jasmine
    lotus
    patchouli
    rose
    ylang-ylang

Prosperity and abundance

Deities to invoke for prosperity and abundance

    Agathodaimon (Greek)
    Ebisu (Japanese)
    Fortuna (Roman)
    Ganesha (Hindu)
    Lakshmi (Hindu)
    Vesunna (Celtic Gaul)

Botanicals for prosperity and abundance

clover
elderflower
garlic
jade plant
oak
pine
thyme

Colours for prosperity and abundance

black (reinforcement)
brown (strength)
red (empowerment)

Crystals and precious stones for prosperity and abundance

amazonite
citrine
emerald
green jade
malachite
pyrite

Essential oils for prosperity and abundance

bergamot
frankincense
ginger
oud
patchouli

Success and self-empowerment

Deities to invoke for success and empowerment
Apollo (Greek)
Artemis (Greek)
Brigid (Celtic)
Cernunnos (Celtic)
Durga (Hindu)
Indra (Hindu)
Isis (Egyptian)
Zeus (Greek)

Botanicals for success and self-empowerment
angelica
bay leaf
birch
ficus
olive leaf
sage
thyme

Colours for success and empowerment
black (integrity)
brown (conviction)
green (manifestation)
red (self-belief)

Crystals and precious stones for success and empowerment

ametrine
carnelian
jet
obsidian
sunstone

Essential oils for success and empowerment

cedarwood
eucalyptus
oud
vetiver

Spiritual growth

Deities to invoke for spiritual growth

Arianrhod (Celtic)
Artemis (Greek)
Hecate (Greek)
Horus (Egyptian)
Selene (Greek)

Botanicals for spiritual growth

ash tree
hibiscus
honeysuckle
lavender
lotus

poppy
water lily

Colours for spiritual growth
blue (intuition)
purple (spiritual awareness)
turquoise (compassion)
white (soul/divine connection)

Crystals and precious stones for spiritual growth
clear quartz
fluorite
labradorite
lapis lazuli
moonstone
turquoise

Essential oils for spiritual growth
cedarwood
clove
cypress
sandalwood

Acknowledgements

I am eternally grateful to everyone at Piatkus, especially Jillian Young and Bernadette Marron, for their magical help in making this book so beautiful. I would also like to thank my agent, Chelsey Fox, my family and friends (you know who you are) for their patience, love and support. Thanks also to my daughter, Jess, for contributing her lovely illustration, 'Fox and Moon' (page 150) – and not forgetting Mother Earth herself, Gaia, who inspired me with words, art and a belief in magical living.